Public Policy
and the Internet

T0164096

The Hoover Institution
gratefully acknowledges generous support from

TAD AND DIANNE TAUBE
TAUBE FAMILY FOUNDATION
KORET FOUNDATION

Founders of the Program on
American Institutions and Economic Performance

and Cornerstone gifts from

SARAH SCAIFE FOUNDATION

Public Policy
and the Internet

Privacy, Taxes,
and Contract

Edited by
Nicholas Imparato

Hoover Institution Press
Stanford University
Stanford, California

www.hoover.org

Hoover Institution Press Publication No. 481

First printing, 2000
07   06   05   04   03   02   9   8   7   6   5   4   3   2

Manufactured in the United States of America

The paper used in this publication meets the minimum requirements
of American National Standard for Information Sciences—Permanence
of Paper for Printed Library Materials, ANSI Z39.48–1984. ⊚

Library of Congress Cataloging-in-Publication Data

Public policy and the Internet : privacy, taxes, and contract / edited by
Nicholas Imparato.
        p.   cm.
    ISBN 0-8179-9892-6 (alk. paper)
    1. Internet (Computer network)—Law and legislation—United States.
2. Electronic commerce—Law and legislation—United States.   3. Electronic
commerce—Taxation—Law and legislation—United States.   4. Contracts—
United States—Data processing.   5. Privacy, Right of—United States.
I. Imparato, Nicholas, 1944–
KF390.5.C6 P83   2000
346.7302′2—dc21   00-026125

Contents

Foreword

The Hoover Institution has long strived to generate ideas defining a free society. The advent of the Internet, a huge development in our society, is a symbol of freedom of information and commerce. It is natural for government to invite itself to consider regulations therein. Thus, it is important that policy thinkers be prepared to articulate the role of government and public policy as this new technology flourishes.

The Hoover Institution takes pride in being a first-class convener of intellectual thinking on public policy concerns. This institutional attribute is easily highlighted given our location in the heart of Silicon Valley. We have access to some of the pioneers of this technology and had an opportunity to convene an important gathering to discuss sweeping issues. Herewith, we present papers by three experts. Earlier versions of these papers led more than twenty leaders of the financial and computing industries to convene at the Hoover Institution to discuss the impact of proposed public policies on Internet communication and commerce.

Hoover research fellow Nicholas Imparato conceived of this project, identified the participants, directed the discussion, and edited this book. This is Imparato's second effort along these lines, having edited *Capital for Our Time: The Economic, Legal, and Management Challenges of Intellectual Capital* (Hoover Press, 1999).

In addition, Associate Director Richard Sousa and Hoover Institution public policy analyst Peter Montgomery deserve acknowledgment for their significant organizational contribution, both conceptually and administratively. Hoover symposia also require the effort of many dedicated staff; I am pleased to thank Kelly Hauge, Teresa Judd, Lea Limgenco, and Craig Snarr for their efforts in this regard.

Finally, and most important, we are deeply grateful to the Charles Schwab Corporation and to Wilson, Sonsini, Goodrich, and Rosati of Palo Alto, California, for their financial support of the symposium and book.

John Raisian
Director
Hoover Institution

Acknowledgments

Richard Sousa, associate director of the Hoover Institution, deserves gratitude for his support of this book and the symposium associated with it. Our discussions regarding topic selection and the structure of the symposium were important in helping the project maintain coherence and focus. I am also indebted to Fred Kittler, cofounder of the Velocity Group, as well as Peter Montgomery, public policy analyst, and John Raisian, director, the Hoover Institution, who provided encouragement along the way and feedback when needed.

Ann Wood, senior editor, and Pat Baker, executive editor, Hoover Institution Press deserve thanks for putting the final copy of the book together. Their effort in turning manuscript to completed volume in an accelerated time frame is especially appreciated.

Finally, the chapter authors and symposium participants showed an earnestness and intellectual honesty throughout the project that earns a special respect. Their sincere commitment to identifying issues and solutions, regardless of their original biases or initial positions, encourages optimism about how policy can be developed for the common good.

Contributors

MARY J. CRONIN is professor of management at Boston College. Her research focuses on electronic commerce issues, international information management, and impact of the net on business strategies. Cronin works as a consultant with Fortune 500 and multinational corporations and serves on the board of several Internet-based start-ups. In addition, she has published numerous books, articles, and case studies on Internet business.

NICHOLAS IMPARATO is a research fellow at the Hoover Institution and professor of management at the University of San Francisco. He is author, coauthor, and editor of numerous publications, including *Jumping the Curve* (Jossey Bass, 1994) and *Capital for Our Time* (Hoover Institution Press, 1999). He is also a contributing editor for *Intelligent Enterprise* magazine and chairman of PrimeWave Solutions.

CHARLES E. MCLURE JR. is a senior fellow at the Hoover Institution. From 1983 to 1985 he was deputy assistant secretary for tax analysis in the U.S. Treasury Department, where he was responsible for developing the proposals to President Ronald Reagan that underlay the Tax Reform Act of 1986, the most thorough reform of the income tax since its inception in 1913.

MARGARET JANE RADIN is the William Benjamin Scott and Luna M. Scott Professor of Law at Stanford University and codirector of Stanford Law School's Program in Law, Science and Technology. Radin teaches and writes about the evolving legal infrastructure of the networked digital environment, focusing on electronic commerce and intellectual property in cyberspace.

Nicholas Imparato

Introduction

In October 1999 a group of promi-
nent executives, Hoover fellows, and academics met to discuss Internet public policy. The initial focus was on privacy and taxation
but eventually came to include, as a function of the interrelation-
ships among the issues, contract and jurisdiction as well. Three
papers framed the discussion. Each constitutes the core of one of
the chapters of this volume.

For the initial chapter, "Privacy and Electronic Commerce,"
Mary J. Cronin surveys opinion and position papers regarding how
to deal with on-line privacy, the meaning of privacy in electronic
commerce, and the arguments between advocates of self-regulation
and legislative models. Her organization and unbiased presentation of the issues, as well as her observations and recommendations

derived from this review, advance an understanding of various alternatives regarding privacy policy.

Charles E. McLure Jr.'s "The Taxation of Electronic Commerce: Background and Proposal" first describes the arguments for and against a tax holiday for Internet commerce, the impediments to equal tax treatment of electronic commerce, and current norms and practices in state sales and national taxation. In the second half of the chapter, McLure departs from this "neutral" survey and outlines his proposals, leading with a single, uniform nationwide base for sales and use taxes, to the Advisory Commission on Electronic Commerce.

Margaret Jane Radin's "Retooling Contract for the Digital Era" evaluates the crisis for contract precipitated by the advent of electronic commerce. She carefully identifies five interrelated problems: authentication, binding commitment, standardization, excluded terms, and jurisdiction and choice of law. By examining "click-wrap" contracts, electronic agents and enforcers, and other elements of the contract environment, Radin leads to a commentary on the broader issues and a reflection on what's at stake.

In short, then, each chapter begins in the fashion of a "white paper," with an objective description of pertinent issues, and then proceeds to present a particular point of view. The common starting point is that policy development should engage the private sector in ways that allow it to contribute meaningfully to the ongoing debates. In this spirit, the authors used the October discussion with peers and executives to sharpen their understanding of the issues and to clarify their own recommendations and conclusions.

Not all differences of opinion were resolved, obviously, during that meeting or subsequent discussions. Yet there were some elements of an emerging consensus or, perhaps, a foundation on which to build a consensus, on the issues of primary focus—privacy and taxation. These points of agreement are important and worth noting even though individual chapter authors eventually proposed recommendations that went beyond the group's conclusions.

For example, there was wide recognition that privacy, as the number one issue of concern for individuals using the web, was most likely to generate emotional debate and thus required a more sophisticated understanding of the dynamics, expectations, and fears associated with threats to it. This understanding, not corporate defensiveness, should be the basis for anticipating problems and developing solutions. Further, the executives and academics concluded that the on-line industry needed to be more proactive in defining what is involved in self-regulation. The kind of self-regulation that exists now in the securities business achieved appreciable support, along with the recognition that government had a key role in assisting industry in this area. All agreed that, given the global reach of the web, the discrepancy between European and American policies needed to be bridged, but how this could be achieved in the face of the European Union's legislative model was unclear. Finally, most agreed that too little of the privacy debate focuses on what benefits the consumer can gain from sharing information and sensitive data. Clearly, consumers need to know how unique characteristics of the web—interactivity, accountability—permit one-to-one marketing and product customization to serve their needs.

A substantial consensus prevailed that all distribution channels—physical presence, mail, telephone, Internet, as well as remote and local sellers—be subject to consistent sales and use taxes. Discussions focused on whether the Internet tax question should be used to reform the current sales tax regime nationwide. Although the group sidestepped a specific recommendation, it generally agreed—again with some difference of opinion still standing—that taking the opportunity occasioned by the rise of e-commerce to reform state sales taxes (first employed in Mississippi in 1932) toward greater simplicity and uniformity would be valuable. Finally, executives and academics agreed that the focus of current debates should be on a destination-based regime for tangible goods. A number of issues surrounding intangible and digital goods still need to be sorted out before a meaningful consensus can be achieved.

An example of a residual issue regarding digital goods was the problem of just how one defines destination in the new, ubiquitous, portable information environment. As in other areas, it was agreed that enhancement of the legal infrastructure—particularly, contract and jurisdiction—for a "clicks and mortar" economy was needed.

Taken together, the symposium discussions held in October and the viewpoints presented here reinforce the judgment that the future of e-commerce will have as much to do with how policy issues are resolved as with how any technological challenge is overcome. Meanwhile, policy in a democracy results from a contest among ideas in free and open debate. In this sense, the resolution of the privacy, taxation, and contract challenges will speak not only to the future of e-commerce but also to the vitality of our fundamental institutions.

Mary J. Cronin

	Privacy and Electronic Commerce
1	

Every opinion and lifestyle variant known to humankind has found a home somewhere on the Internet, so it should come as no surprise that the global network has also spawned diverse and deeply held positions on the subject of on-line privacy. It might seem that the very nature of the net, with its open participation and millions of entry points around the globe, runs counter to many traditional notions about privacy. But labeling "Internet privacy" an oxymoron is not likely to end the debate. The explosion of web sites actively collecting, mining, and sharing information about individual Internet users has prompted a serious policy division between those countries (notably the United States) that support self-regulation of Internet privacy practices and those that have enacted government measures to protect

With thanks to Joseph Jose, Boston College MBA '01, for his valuable assistance in gathering and analyzing the background materials for this chapter.

personal data. Privacy has also emerged as a touchstone for consumer concerns about the Internet, fueled by media revelations of behind-the-scenes web data collection practices.

This chapter discusses the major issues that have emerged in the debate over on-line privacy, with a particular focus on the differences between the regulatory outlook in the United States and that in the European Union. It raises three related policy questions:

- Is the appropriate balance between privacy and information disclosure best negotiated between the individual users and the web sites they choose to visit or is some type of regulation or external review required to improve current privacy practices?

- Does the U.S. reliance on corporate self-regulation put it on a collision course with the European Union and other regions that have opted for government-enforced privacy protection standards?

- Would insistence on protecting the privacy of individual information collected via the web promote on-line business growth by boosting consumer confidence in electronic commerce, or is it more likely to constrain competition on the net and stifle entrepreneurial opportunities?

To help answer these questions, the chapter synthesizes a growing body of published opinion, survey results, and position papers on the central issues posed by privacy on the web:

- The challenges of defining information privacy in the context of electronic commerce

- The pros and cons of private sector self-regulation in comparison to government-led policy and legislation in dealing with on-line privacy and the treatment of personal information on the Internet

- The forces that are influencing corporate self-regulation in the United States and the impact of these forces on web privacy practices to date

I conclude that the critical issue is more fundamental than the debate over government regulation versus self-regulation of on-line privacy. Even more important is the short-term value that companies place on unreported collection of user information compared to the longer-term value of building customer trust. The Internet is awash in information, but trust is still in short supply and high demand. Linking privacy best practices to the premium placed on trusted on-line relationships, educating the public about how to make intelligent choices about information disclosure, and continuing to expose the covert collection of on-line user information by any company are essential in order for privacy and electronic commerce to coexist.

Changing the Parameters of Privacy

Information privacy concerns have, of course, accompanied the adoption of many technology innovations that are now part of our daily lives. Mass circulation newspapers have combined with the telegraph and telephone to feed an age-old curiosity about the rich and famous with late-breaking gossip news. In fact, the intrusive behavior of the press over a century ago inspired a landmark *Harvard Law Review* article by Samuel D. Warren and Louis D. Brandeis that defined the essence of privacy as "the right of the individual to be let alone."[1] In 1928, as a Supreme Court justice, Louis Brandeis dissented to the Court's support of another technology—government wiretaps—to underscore his conviction that privacy

1. "The Right to Privacy," *Harvard Law Review* 193, 1890.

was "the most comprehensive of rights and the right most valued by civilized men."[2]

Long before the Internet became a household word, it was clear that celebrities and criminals were not the only citizens subject to scrutiny. The everyday activities of most Americans are now routinely recorded and analyzed by a variety of governmental and commercial organizations. From telephone calls to ATM withdrawals and credit card purchases, from supermarket discount cards to doctors' visits and drivers' licenses, we generate data with almost every move we make. Collection and analysis of that data trigger a variety of incursions on our "right to be let alone," from piles of advertising in our mailboxes to phone solicitations at the dinner hour to audit flags on our income tax returns.

Detailed information on an individual's credit, health, and financial status, on characteristic purchasing patterns, and on other personal preferences is readily available on centralized computer databases and is the engine behind the multibillion-dollar direct marketing industry. A May 1999 survey on privacy in *The Economist* notes that "the trade in consumer information has hugely expanded in the past ten years. One single company, Axicom Corporation in Conway, Arkansas, has a database combining public and consumer information that covers 95% of American households."[3] A *Forbes* cover story in November 1999, "I Know What You Did Last Night," highlights the way different slices of consumer data can now be pulled together to create a composite picture of any individual's life. "Computers now hold half a billion bank accounts, half a billion credit card accounts, hundreds of millions of mortgages and retirement funds and medical claims and more. The web seamlessly links it all together. As e-commerce

2. Quoted in Robert Ellis Smith, ed., *Compilation of State & Federal Privacy Laws* (Providence, R.I.: Privacy Journal, 1997), p. v.
3. "The End of Privacy," *The Economist*, May 1, 1999, p. 21.

grows, marketers and busybodies will crack open a cache of new consumer data more revealing than ever before."[4]

To provide some controls on the maintenance of such data, and to give citizens a chance to review and correct potentially damaging conclusions about creditworthiness and employability, Congress and state governments enacted a series of consumer protection laws and guidelines starting in the 1970s. The first, the Fair Credit Reporting Act of 1970, spells out requirements for credit investigation companies to give public notice of their information collection activities and to provide subjects with an opportunity to review and comment on information about themselves. The Cable Communications Policy Act of 1984 applies even more rigorous standards to the protection of personal information about cable service subscribers. Cable providers cannot collect personal information about subscribers without their explicit consent and must provide explicit opt-out opportunities even for mailing lists that are not directly related to providing cable services. Information that is no longer needed in order to provide service must be destroyed by the cable operator in a timely fashion. This act protects consumers from having their cable providers track (and resell) information about their viewing habits and preferences and provides for subscribers who feel their privacy has been violated to sue for damages. Even more rigorous criminal law penalties are attached to the Video Privacy Act of 1998 that protects records about personal rental of videos. Individuals must give explicit written permission (opt-in) to share this information outside the original purpose for which it was collected.

A number of states have adopted similar principles for oversight and access to governmental and private databases about individual residents. The state of California includes an article in its state constitution recognizing the right to privacy, and many states

4. "I Know What You Did Last Night" *Forbes*, November 29, 1999, p. 183.

have passed laws or issued regulations protecting specific types of information including telephone calling patterns, health and financial records. More recently, New York and other states have considered legislation to protect on-line privacy for consumers. Despite this array of existing legislation, the amount of personal consumer information that is routinely collected and stored continues to increase dramatically from year to year. As the amount of data skyrockets and the software tools to profile and analyze that information become more sophisticated and readily available, the risks associated with unwanted exposure or inappropriate access to sensitive elements of those data are also on the rise.

Even though most of the personal information in question has come from interactions with banks, credit card associations, direct mail houses, and other organizations that started mining personal data for profit long before the net burst into prominence, public concern about privacy protection today tends to focus on the Internet. If our society and its citizens have been living with pervasive personal data collection over the past several decades, why has the Internet become such a focal point for concerns about individual privacy? Are we holding the Internet up to a standard of privacy protection that has been abandoned in our dealings with other media? In answering this question it is useful to consider how the Internet challenges traditional notions of privacy and how different disciplines are attempting to address the difficulties of protecting and even of defining what constitutes personal privacy in the context of a multifunctional, easily customizable, and still evolving global network.

The Eyes of the Beholders

Here is a self-administered privacy test that is frequently used to illustrate the spectrum of opinion on what constitutes a privacy issue in different settings:

Imagine that you are spending the afternoon at a shopping mall, partly browsing but also intending to purchase a number of things that reflect your individual interests and needs—everything from videos and books to gifts, to a prescription refill and some personal hygiene items. Unbeknownst to you, a marketing firm has hired someone to follow you around, recording everything you look at, noting any questions you ask, what you select for purchase, and how you pay for it. As you are about to leave the mall, this person approaches you with an offer for a discount on future purchases that makes you suspect that all your activities have been closely monitored.

What is your reaction to the discount offer? Would you be happy to take the discount with no questions about how it was tailored to your interests? Would you demand to know more about what information the observer had collected and what would be done with it? Would you feel that this type of surreptitious observation was less of a service and more of an unwanted intrusion on your privacy? Now shift the focus of the scenario to browsing and buying on the web. Does this change your reaction to the discount offer?

There are no consistent answers to these questions, and the wide range of reaction mirrors the different ideas that people have about private/public boundaries and comfort levels with sharing personal information. Before the Internet, the scenario and the responses to it might have been of academic interest in defining privacy boundaries, but they would not have had much real-life application. Following customers around on their shopping excursions was not financially viable for companies in the physical world, so they relied on other, more cost-effective, means of consumer profiling and data collection. Tracking shopper's behavior on the Internet is, however, efficient and increasingly common. Instead of contemplating a hypothetical scenario, on-line consumers face the reality of constant scrutiny.

The real-time application of information collection, behavior monitoring, and data-mining activities has been significantly enhanced by the Internet, enabling new approaches to interactive marketing and the personalization of advertising messages through a variety of new media tools and technologies. Sophisticated on-line tools enable even the smallest companies to obtain and analyze types of customer information that were previously impossible to compile or available only to those corporations with massive marketing budgets. Gartner Group predicts that 85 percent of the world's largest companies will have an active on-line marketing program by the end of 2000. These programs typically include the ability to track the path that on-line users take through the company's own web site, what documents the user opens, what searches take place, how long a user spends on any part of the site, and what items are placed into shopping carts. All this data can then be linked to whatever personal information the user may have shared with the company by filling out a registration form, requesting a special service, and so on.

Many users are not aware that their on-line behavior is so readily recorded and analyzed. Even fewer know that services like DoubleClick contract with a number of the most popular web sites to pool on-line browsing information for an even richer and more detailed profile of consumer behavior across all of its clients. When DoubleClick announced plans in the summer of 1999 to acquire Abacus Direct, an off-line database-marketing company, privacy advocates quickly raised objections. They asserted that merging the Abacus database—an enormous file with individual names, addresses, and buying patterns of more than 88 million catalog shoppers—with the on-line tracking power of DoubleClick would concentrate too much personal consumer information in the hands of one company. DoubleClick does not currently link its on-line behavior profile services to individual names and addresses, but the merger raised the possibility of future products with even more detailed personal reports. Despite a flurry of criticism and discussion in public policy and privacy circles, the merger announcement and its implications for on-line privacy never penetrated the general consumer consciousness. One reason is that the techniques and technologies that underpin both on-line tracking and personalization service are still mysterious to the average Internet user. Another is that DoubleClick and similar services operate behind the scenes, and, unlike the decision to fill out a form on a web site, their data-gathering activity never becomes visible to the average Internet user.

For the hundreds of companies that develop and market such on-line tracking and data-mining capabilities, the development of these technologies and their adoption by millions of web sites represent vital entrepreneurial opportunities. Clearly, these on-line data-tracking and analysis products are much in demand. For all types of companies that do business on the web, learning as much as possible about visitors is a precondition for offering customized services and may be the key to growth and expanded revenues. Unless there is some external pressure to place limits on how much customer information is collected, or how it is used, it seems likely that on-line data-mining practices will be fine-tuned and expanded as quickly as the technology that supports them.

If companies on the Internet continue to soak up information as fast as customers can click through a web site, then privacy will be hostage to technology. A small percentage of web-savvy and technically astute users may register their objections and find ways to subvert those practices they define as a violation of their privacy. Small groups of consumers may adopt the new tools and services that are emerging to provide on-line anonymity by serving as a single trusted proxy for the individual. Others may have no problems with full disclosure to any web site and may simply wish to be informed in advance that tracking is taking place. In the absence of any accepted guidelines clarifying the scope of acceptable data collection or regulation limiting the use of personal information, questions about the appropriate balance of privacy and disclosure would have to be weighed by the individual consumer and then negotiated with each web site that is visited. Even a brief review of legal, ethical, economic, and philosophical approaches to the issue of privacy protection will illustrate that this type of negotiation is likely to be a daunting proposition.

From the ethical and the legal perspective, it is important to establish whether the Internet is intrinsically a public place—that is, a location where it is clear to users that their actions and communications can be readily observed. The flexibility of the Internet and the multiple functions that it serves for most users make the answer less obvious than it might initially appear. Many users understand that their participation in a chat room or a query to a popular search engine or clicking on a banner ad is likely to be observed and recorded. But what about their registration on a financial information services web page or their on-line purchases or their one-to-one messages. Are these subject to the same level of scrutiny and onward transfer?

The Internet is well known for openness and information leakage, providing support for the argument that individuals have no reason to expect that their communications and behavior will remain private. But often our interactions with the net do have a private feel to them. Users are alone with their computers and involved in what seems to be a real-time dialogue with a particular web site rather than a multiparty conversation that will be recorded and forwarded to points unknown. In fact, the web tracking and data capture mechanisms are deliberately designed to be transparent to the user, and the more sophisticated the technology becomes, the less of a footprint it will leave on the desktop.

As long as Internet users visit a web site knowing that they are in a public space where monitoring of behavior and personal data collection does not violate any norms, they should not expect their actions to remain confidential. The body of existing legal precedent in the United States leans toward putting the responsibility on the individual to take some explicit action to restrict the reuse of personal information once it has been voluntarily disclosed. For example, if a consumer decides to fill out and submit a detailed questionnaire about buying habits or taste in music in order to receive a discount or token gift, that individual cannot reasonably assume that the information submitted will be kept confidential. In fact, blanket restrictions on the reuse of such information are seen as placing limits on the freedom of speech of the original recipient.

There are counterarguments, however. Answering questions about one's health history or medical information interests on a web site that is dedicated to providing support and resources for a specific health problem is likely to seem logical and reasonably private. An individual may have no reason to think that the information he or she provides could well become part of a larger personal profile of on-line behavior that will be stored and accessible to third parties for years to come. She or he would be unlikely to imagine that information is being forwarded on the spot to a totally different web site that specializes in insurance coverage. If consumers did realize that this long-term storage and onward transfer was going to happen, they might think more carefully about balancing the value of the resources they receive from the health site with the disclosure of personal information. The definition of the Internet as fully public rather than semiprivate is an important distinction to make since legal opinion tends to be built on the reasonable expectations that individuals have about how their information will be handled. A number of scholars have pointed out that defining the very notion of reasonable expectations is complicated, even without taking the Internet into account. As Judith DeCew notes:[5]

5. Judith Wagner DeCew, *In Pursuit of Privacy: Law, Ethics, and the Rise of Technology* (Ithaca, N.Y., and London: Cornell University Press), p. 21.

Because there is no right to privacy explicitly guaranteed in the Constitution and because the constitutional cases regarding this right are so diverse, there has been a great deal of criticism and controversy surrounding this right to privacy. It is even more difficult to describe than the informational privacy protected in tort and Fourth Amendment law.

Economists take a different approach, suggesting that on-line privacy rights be defined in the context of personal property. In this framework all the personal information about an individual belongs to that person, and he or she should be free to protect or dispose of it as desired. Since the information has value on-line, the individual is entitled to make a choice to trade it or sell it for an agreed-on compensation.[6] In this context, the essence of privacy protection is having control over what happens to information about oneself. Individuals must have the ability to grant as well as to deny access to personal information on the Internet; thus regulations that preempt the individual's choice to disclose all personal data may in fact limit the full exercise of privacy rights. Although this approach accommodates the diversity of individual positions on privacy, it raises a number of difficulties in terms of implementation, feasibility, and consistency of definition.

In practice, implementing such a solution would require some prior legal or regulatory action to establish a clear link between individual information and personal property rights. This legal area is fraught with complexity and unlikely to develop a consensus among all the potential players anytime soon. The logic of equating privacy with property also implies that one could reveal absolutely everything about oneself (for the right price) and still be considered to have held onto the essence of privacy. From a philosophical point of view, however, this extreme would change the

6. Richard Posner, *The Economics of Justice* (Cambridge, Mass.: Harvard University Press, 1983).

terms of the dialogue from privacy protection to the realm of autonomy and freedom of choice.

A philosophical framework for defining on-line privacy advanced by James Moor is grounded in the principles of individual control and freedom of choice about personal information.[7] Moor distinguishes between situations that can be considered "normatively" private, where privacy is protected by ethical or legal norms, and situations that are "naturally" private. In normatively private situations, sexual intimacy, for example, or client-attorney consultation, unwanted observation and recording of behavior is a clear violation of privacy. In cases of natural privacy individuals may happen to be unobserved because of the situation or location they are in, but a loss of that privacy does not constitute an intrusion because there are no clear norms dictating that the situation should not be publicly accessible. Moor suggests that there is no normative privacy on the Internet but that users should be able to exercise informed consent about how much data is collected about them and in what situations such data can be used.

On-line privacy issues are intrinsically complex because they represent an intersection of legal, commercial, governmental, ethical, philosophical, and personal positions. It is highly unlikely that any one policy or law will manage to address all these perspectives and provide a universally satisfactory resolution to the problem when the very definition of Internet privacy is still open to debate. Rapid changes in technology and a lack of consensus on basic definitions typically indicate that a strict set of regulations is likely to miss the mark and instead create cumbersome results. But the pressure is on to take more positive steps to encourage consistent commercial privacy protections across the Internet. The fact that the U.S. stance on self-regulation is out of step with government and

---

7. James Moor, "Towards a Theory of Privacy in the Information Age," *Computers and Society*, September 1997, pp. 27–32.

public sector initiatives in Europe and elsewhere is only one of the factors driving change. Closer to home, many studies of consumer attitudes report that U.S. consumers are worried about what will happen to the information that they create when they register for services or surf the web. This combination of factors has added an element of urgency to the long-running academic and legal discussions about privacy protection in general and has raised immediate issues for how governments, corporations, and individuals interact over the collection of personal information on the Internet.

Current Consumer Privacy Perceptions

A number of surveys document that consumers do indeed see the use of the Internet as a potential threat to their privacy. A 1997 study of 9,300 Internet users by the Boston Consulting Group reported that more than 70 percent of the respondents were more concerned about privacy on the Internet than they were about privacy threats from any other medium. A joint *Business Week*/Harris survey in 1998 identified concern about personal privacy as the number one consumer issue related to use of the net. A survey of experienced Internet users sponsored by AT&T Labs reported that 87 percent of the respondents were concerned about threats to their privacy on-line. The issues cited by consumers in these studies are similar to the different disciplines' efforts to pinpoint the essence of information privacy on the Internet. Consumers mention the lack of clarity about how information collected on-line may be used, confusion about the privacy implications of web site practices based on new technology (such as tracking clickstreams or setting cookies), and objections about information collected at one web site being shared with third parties. Consumers are also aware of certain Internet characteristics, which underscore their feeling that using the net may put their personal information at risk. These include

- Difficulty in determining who to trust when confronted with a large, heterogeneous group of companies doing business on-line, many of which do not have any bricks-and-mortar presence or reputation

- The general perception that web sites have greatly enhanced the ability to collect, mine, and correlate information from multiple sources to create a detailed individual profile

- Confusion about how on-line profiling of personal preferences and onward transfer actually takes place and where the information collected on one site may eventually be stored and accessed

- Lack of any centralized governing structure to take responsibility or assume liability for privacy and other violations by individual web sites

Although it is impossible to measure precisely, such widely held privacy concerns are likely to negatively affect the growth of electronic commerce. According to some analysts the majority of consumers are holding back on Internet purchases primarily because they worry about potential privacy abuses. Despite the fact that millions of Internet users have already purchased items on the net, these studies suggest that browsing and buying levels would be much higher if consumers were confident that personal information would be safeguarded on-line. The finding that experienced Internet users (as polled in the AT&T-sponsored survey) expressed at least as much concern as nonusers or new users suggests that perceived privacy threats are not just the result of unfamiliarity with the network.

What do these survey results imply for the questions raised at the beginning of this chapter? The persistence of consumer concerns over time and the heterogeneous, dynamic nature of millions of small on-line businesses weigh against the free market position that "the appropriate balance between privacy and information disclosure [is] best negotiated between the individual user and the web sites they choose to visit." Peter Swire points out a number of questions that can help establish the likely effectiveness of free market forces in changing Internet business practices:[8]

1. How difficult is it for consumers to discover companies' policies for use of private information and monitor the companies' compliance with those policies?

2. How much do such difficulties lead to overuse of private information by companies?

3. How difficult is it for consumers who wish to do so to bargain with companies for different privacy practices?

Swire concludes that, given current Internet business practices, consumers would pay too high a price in time and convenience to determine and monitor the privacy policies of every company they may want to visit on the web. The ability of companies to avoid such scrutiny in turn makes it likely that they will use the consumer information available to them in ways that may have little relationship to the purpose for which it was originally collected. Consumers have little recourse via individual bargaining, and the size, fluidity, and heterogeneity of the merchant and user community on the net make it unlikely that the majority of merchants with objectionable privacy and information collection practices will be effectively penalized by the marketplace.

The combination of widespread consumer concern about Internet privacy threats and the barriers to the operation of free market forces to regulate on-line business practices seems to argue for

8. Peter Swire, "Markets, Self-Regulation, and Government Enforcement in the Protection of Personal Information," from the Peter Swire Home Page, www.acs.Ohio-State.edu/units/law/swire1/pshome1.htl.

more aggressive action to ensure privacy. If improvements in on-line privacy protection are needed, and market competition alone is unlikely to stimulate them, then a move toward stronger articulation of best-practices privacy models and regular outside scrutiny of on-line data-gathering practices is arguably the appropriate next step. But even among those who agree on the need for some kind of regulatory effort, there is a deep division between proponents of self-regulation by companies and those who believe that government action and enforcement are required to ensure meaningful compliance from on-line businesses. This division is embodied most clearly in the regulatory situation in the United States versus that in the European Union. The next section discusses the major differences between the United States and the European Union and analyzes the pros and cons of the two positions.

Two Cultures: Voluntary and Regulated Consumer Data Protection

On-line privacy protection seems to look very different from the two sides of the Atlantic. Note the contrast in the following statements.

As noted in the Commission's 1998 Report, self-regulation is the least intrusive and most efficient means to ensure fair information practices, given the rapidly evolving nature of the Internet and computer technology. During the past year the Commission has been monitoring self-regulatory initiatives to address the privacy concerns of on-line consumers. In some areas, there has been much progress. (*Self-Regulation and Privacy On-line, A Report to Congress*, Federal Trade Commission, July 1999)

Whereas the object of the national laws on the processing of personal data is to protect fundamental rights and freedoms, notably the right to privacy, which is recognized both in Article 8 of the European Convention for the Protection of Human Rights and Fundamental Freedoms and in the general principles of Community law; whereas, for that reason, the approximation of those laws must not result in any lessening of the protection they afford but must, on the contrary, seek to ensure a high level of protection in the Community,

1. In accordance with this Directive, Member States shall protect the fundamental rights and freedoms of natural persons, and in particular their right to privacy with respect to the processing of personal data. (Chapter 1, Article 1, *European Directive on Data Protection*)

The European Union (EU) has focused on aligning national laws of its member states to ensure consistent protection for European citizens' personal information. As many analysts have pointed out, this approach reflects a tradition of government protection and oversight of individual data collection on behalf of citizens. European governments tend toward more stringent regulation of corporate activities than the United States, which favors self-regulation by the private sector when possible. In addition, Europe's historical experience with fascist and communist regimes has heightened national sensitivities about the potential for abuse from monitoring individual behavior and compiling detailed information files.

The specific regulations articulated in the European Directive on Data Protection that went into force in October 1998 highlight these cultural and political differences and present a direct challenge to common electronic commerce practices of U.S. corporations. Not only has the EU promulgated restrictions on how its member state companies can collect and share customer information in electronic form, but it has also taken a preemptive stab at enforcing these regulations outside its own borders. Particularly controversial is the EU stance that these same protections must remain in force when European citizens' data are collected or transmitted to any database anywhere in the world.

This aspect of the directive has sweeping implications that extend far beyond electronic commerce practices. A recent book on the impact of the directive details more than thirty major business activities, from human resource files to faxes, that are covered by the directive. "The Directive is sweeping in scope, applying to all 'processing' of personal data, with only limited exceptions. Processing is a broad term that means 'any operation or set of operations which is performed upon personal data, whether or not by automatic means.' Personal data is a similarly broad term, meaning 'any information relating to an identified or identifiable natural person (data subject).'"[9]

It remains to be seen whether the EU will actively attempt to enforce the directive internationally and will bring charges against entities in the United States or elsewhere that do not demonstrate adequate compliance with all of its regulations. Two factors are worth noting. First, the directive does explicitly give enforcement authorities in each member state "investigative powers," "effective powers of intervention," and "the power to engage in legal proceedings." Second, as of September 1999, the EU has determined that the current Safe Harbor Principles established by the U.S. Department of Commerce to guide voluntary compliance by corporations do not comply with the standard of "adequate protection" prescribed by the directive. One significant area of noncompliance is the lack of enforcement authority for U.S. web privacy practices.

Table 1 highlights the specific provisions of the EU privacy directive that relate to on-line data collection practices that are common in the United States. Column 1 provides a general

9. Peter P. Swire and Robert E. Litan, *None of Your Business: World Data Flows, Electronic Commerce, and the European Privacy Directive* (Washington, D.C.: Brookings Institution Press, 1998).

TABLE I
European Union Privacy Directive Provisions

Provision Description	Applicable Section of the Directive
When collecting information from an individual, those processing data (known as the *controllers*) must disclose their identities, the purposes for the processing, and other information.	Section IV: "Information to be given to the data subject" Article 10: a) the identity of the controller of his representative, if any b) the purposes of the processing for which the data are intended c) any further information such as • the recipients or categories of recipients of the data • whether replies to the questions are obligatory or voluntary, as well as the possible consequences of failure to reply • the existence of the right of access to and the right to rectify the data concerning him
Data can be processed only for the purposes that have been announced, must be kept up to date, and may not be kept linked to individual identity for longer than needed for the original purposes.	Article 6 (1): Personal data must be: a) processed fairly and lawfully b) collected for a specified, explicit and legitimate purpose and not further processed in a way incompatible with those purposes c) adequate, relevant and not excessive in relation to the purposes for which they are collected d) accurate and, where necessary, kept up to date e) kept in a form which permits identification of data subjects for no longer than is necessary for the purposes for which the data were collected
Before data can be provided to third parties for direct marketing, the individual must be informed and have the right to opt out at no cost.	14 (b) to be informed before personal data are disclosed for the first time to third parties or used on their behalf for the purposes of direct marketing, and to be expressly offered the right to object free of charge to such disclosures or uses.

TABLE I

(*continued*)

Provision Description	Applicable Section of the Directive
Those processing personal data must guarantee that individuals have access to their own personal data and the opportunity to correct that data.	Section V: The Data Subject's Right of Access to Data: Article 12: a) without constraint at reasonable intervals and without excessive delay or expense • confirmation as to whether or not data relating to him are being processed • communication to him in an intelligible form of the data undergoing processing and of any available information as to their source b) as appropriate the rectification, erasure or blocking of data the processing of which does not comply with the provisions of this Directive, in particular because of the incomplete or inaccurate nature of the data
Transfers of data outside the EU are permitted only if the receiving country ensures an adequate level of privacy protection.	Article 25: Transfer of personal data to third countries . . . may take place only if, without prejudice to compliance with the national provisions adopted pursuant to the other provisions of this Directive, the third country in question ensures an adequate level of protection.
Additional restrictions apply to data considered to be sensitive; this includes racial or ethnic origin, political opinions, health information and sexual practices unless such collection is explicitly exempted.	Article 8: Member states shall prohibit the processing of personal data revealing racial or ethnic origin, political opinions, religious or philosophical beliefs, trade-union membership, and the processing of data concerning health or sex life.

description of the regulation, and column 2 cites language from the relevant article.

Despite the complexity of the directive and the concern about its impact on business practices outside the European Union, the advocates for government regulation to protect on-line privacy project a number of positive outcomes from this approach. Among the most frequently mentioned advantages are

- Consistency in the definition of privacy protection and in the requirements for development of appropriate on-line business practices
- Avoidance of a patchwork of potentially conflicting regulations and privacy positions by different stakeholders within the EU
- Clarity on the total scope of the requirements and corporate reporting responsibilities, which makes it easier for businesses to comply
- Effective means of enforcement
- Increase in consumer confidence in electronic commerce

Opponents of government regulation, however, are quick to point out the negative side of relying on legislation or directives to protect on-line privacy. Arguments raised against such an approach include

- Cumbersome and inflexible, not a good match for the rapid evolution of electronic commerce and web business practices
- Adds burdensome layer of complexity to enterprise, especially small- and medium-size on-line companies
- Could become a significant barrier to on-line start-ups

- Difficult or impossible to enforce around the globe; nature of the net will allow violators to escape

- Does not take enough advantage of the experience of on-line companies

- May not serve or represent the interests of all citizens since some may want to disclose information in exchange for enhanced services or direct compensation

The privacy directive may even fall short in achieving one of its primary goals, the harmonization of privacy protection practice and enforcement throughout the European Union so that the rights of all European citizens would be protected equally. The EU has left it up to each national government to establish the specific laws and enforcement mechanisms that will bring it into compliance with the directive: "Each Member State shall provide that one or more public authorities are responsible for monitoring the application within its territory of the provisions adopted by the Member States pursuant to this Directive: These authorities shall act with complete independence in exercising the functions entrusted to them" (Article 28). The complexity of the directive makes it likely that there will be different interpretations of its provisions among the member states, especially as new developments in electronic commerce create situations that were not envisioned by the original regulations.

Despite these objections to regulation by legislation, the EU is far from alone in opting for strong government action as the best way to ensure that individual privacy and consumer data will be protected on the Internet. Dozens of countries, including Australia and Singapore, have adopted privacy protection laws specifically addressing electronic commerce practices and prohibiting certain types of data collection by companies on the Internet. In fact, the United States is more of an anomaly in relying so strongly on self-regulation to protect privacy rights. Before analyzing the results of this approach from the point of view of current on-line privacy practice in the United States, let us look at the general arguments in favor of self-regulation and a summary of the pros and cons of this approach.

Since the privatization of the Internet in the early 1990s and the subsequent explosion of commercial applications and global user base, the U.S. government has looked favorably on private sector leadership in developing electronic commerce and has urged other countries to do the same. The 1997 Framework For Electronic Commerce states that "commerce on the Internet could total billions of dollars by the turn of the century. For this potential to be realized fully, governments must adopt a non-regulatory, market-oriented approach to electronic commerce, one that facilitates the emergence of a transparent and predictable environment to support global business and commerce."[10]

The goals for global expansion of electronic commerce articulated in 1997 for the turn of the century have already been exceeded, and the U.S. economy has certainly been a beneficiary. As the acknowledged leader in building an infrastructure for electronic commerce and harnessing the Internet for business advantage, the United States has every reason to continue to rely on industry rather than government to take the lead in directing the development of Internet business practices. It is difficult to argue with such stunning success. At the same time, it is reasonable to ask if policies to protect individual on-line privacy belong in the same category as Internet infrastructure or technical standards. Is self-regulation by industry in the United States likely to be more or less effective than the government-enforced protection enacted by the European Union?

10. "A Framework for Global Electronic Commerce," President William J. Clinton and Vice President Albert Gore Jr., Washington, D.C., July 1997

Arguments in favor of self-regulation include

- Is consistent with the overall U.S. stance on the development of the Internet
- Brings industry expertise to bear on solving complex issues
- Promotes flexible and dynamic solutions that can change along with the Internet
- Encourages buy-in from business
- Reflects a better understanding of the implications of implementation and enforcement
- Is proving to be effective as more and more companies adopt recommended privacy practices

In his draft article (on his home page) "Of Elephants, Mice, and Privacy: International Choice of Law and the Internet," Peter Swire provides another rationale for favoring flexible self-regulation over national legislation to protect on-line privacy. Noting that there are two very different types of corporations doing business on the Internet today, he characterizes them as "elephants" and "mice." "Elephants are large, powerful, and practically impossible to hide. Consider a transnational corporation that has major operations in a country. If that country has strict regulations, the corporations' actions will be highly visible and it may become an enforcement target if it flouts the law." As would be expected, the largest corporations have already taken steps to comply with the European Union Directive, and they are models for adopting clear privacy protection practices in the United States.

There are, however, many more mice than elephants on the Internet today, and these small, nimble companies have a number of ways to avoid the consequences of ignoring government sanctions. "At the other extreme, it will be extremely difficult for national regulators to effectively govern data processing by the mice of the electronic world. Many web sites are run by individuals or small companies. . . . Even if jurisdiction is established, there may be no effective way to identify or punish the wrongdoers. Individual users might reveal personal information to such a site, perhaps due to a fraudulent promise to keep information confidential or under the mistaken impression that the site will comply with data protection laws."[11]

Web companies that are not ethical in their practices are going to be difficult and expensive for government regulators to track down and prosecute. Unless consumers are educated enough to consistently avoid doing business with sites that do not prove their privacy policy compliance, any questionable sites that are shut down will soon be replaced by others. The existence of national legislation and the expectation of effective government enforcement of privacy protections might actually lull consumers into a false sense of security in entrusting their confidential information to any web site.

The most negative impact of strict government regulation and record reporting requirements is likely to be felt by the well-meaning middle-size companies and the entrepreneurial start-ups that could be forced to spend a disproportionate amount of time and effort on data monitoring and reporting. Even more broadly, the strategies and business practices of countless sites that collect personal information to customize services or to improve processes would be disrupted. There would be fewer avenues to support the growth of new on-line enterprises and possibly more cumbersome reporting and compliance procedures for documenting privacy protection practices that would be particularly burdensome for small, fast-growing companies.

11. Peter Swire, "Markets."

A number of arguments challenge the effectiveness of self-regulation. These include

- Business models and revenue streams built on divulging personal information collected on web sites will be difficult to dislodge through voluntary compliance once they become entrenched.

- Many existing web privacy statements are inaccurate or fail to comply with recommended practices, and enforcement is difficult without central regulation.

- Consumers should be entitled to the same levels of privacy protection on the Internet that they already receive on cable television.

- In the absence of any congressional action, states may step in and develop local legislation that will make things even more confusing in terms of compliance requirements.

One pressing argument against U.S. reliance on self-regulation is that the European Union is likely to continue challenging the adequacy of U.S. data protection practices unless the government takes a more active role in enforcement. It is not desirable or effective in the long run to compromise on a deeply held belief in self-regulation in order to avoid confrontation with another government. But on a pragmatic level, a direct confrontation with the EU about privacy protection could be a major setback for the global expansion of electronic commerce. Is there a way to come to terms with EU requirements without compromising on the principles and the flexibility that have fostered U.S. success in electronic commerce? This section concludes with a more detailed look at the key differences between the EU directive and the guidelines for on-line privacy protection that have been jointly endorsed by the U.S. government and the private sector.

A 1996 book entitled *Data Privacy Law: A Study of United States Data Protection*, by Paul M. Schwartz and Joel R. Reidenberg, pinpointed four key factors that characterize the European approach to privacy protection as expressed in the privacy directive:[12]

1. The creation of norms for collection and processing of personal information

2. The establishment of an opportunity for affected individuals both to review information collected about themselves and to review the compiler's information practices

3. The creation of special protection for sensitive data such as data pertaining to ethnic origin, political opinions, health and sexual practices

4. The establishment of enforcement mechanisms and oversight systems to ensure the data protection principles are respected

These four factors are quite close to the five core "fair information practice principles" for privacy protection that the U.S. government has established as models for itself and for the private sector in dealing with the collection and on-line maintenance of personal consumer data:

1. Notice/Awareness: consumers must be given notice of a company's information practices before personal information is collected from them

2. Choice/Consent: consumers must be given options with

---

12. Paul M. Schwartz and Joel R. Reidenberg, *Data Privacy Law: A Study of United States Data Protection* (New York: Lexis Law Publications, 1996).

respect to whether and how personal information collected from them must be used

3. Access/Participation: consumers must be given reasonable access to information collected about them and the ability to contest that data's accuracy and completeness

4. Integrity/Security: companies must take reasonable steps to assure that information collected from consumers is accurate and secure from unauthorized use

5. Enforcement/Redress: government and/or self-regulatory mechanisms must be in place to impose sanctions for non-compliance with fair information practices

From this broad perspective, the U.S. government has a strong track record for action on the first factor—establishing norms for personal data collection—stretching back to the 1970 legislation on fair credit reporting. It has also supported the requirements for individual review and correction of credit records, particularly in areas such as educational and medical records. There are provisions for special protection of certain types of records, and the 1998 proposal for congressional action to safeguard the privacy of children on the Internet demonstrates a continuing openness to extra protection for sensitive data. Legal action tends to be the ultimate recourse for rectification of data protection violations, but there are also government agencies to deal with complaints about fraud or misrepresentation of business practices. In other words, there are no fundamental contradictions between the principles laid out by the EU directive and those already in place in U.S. law regarding data and information protection.

This is of course the same line of reasoning that U.S. representatives have presented to the European Union in an attempt to establish that this country already has implemented reasonably adequate protections for on-line data protection and therefore is in compliance with the EU directive. Since these attempts have not been successful to date, it is useful to review some of the specific differences between U.S. practice in Internet privacy protection and the strict interpretation of the EU regulations.

The major differences between the U.S. approach to protecting on-line privacy, defined by the Safe Harbor Principles, and the European Union's privacy policies are the methods of oversight and enforcement, individuals' access to files, and the ability of individuals to stop the sale and use of their personal information. The following explains the similarities and differences based on the issues of notice, choice, onward transfer, security, data integrity, access, and enforcement as outlined in the EU directive.

Notice and Choice

The European Union Directive and the Safe Harbor Principles are similar in handling notice and choice. Both policies state that before individuals are asked to provide information to an organization, they must be informed of the purpose for collecting the data, how to contact the organization, the choices that are available to them, and the means the organization offers individuals for limiting the use and disclosure of the information.

Onward Transfer

There is a subtle difference between the United States and the EU in the policies regarding onward transfer. The directive explicitly states that the individual must be made aware of the processing of personal data for the purposes of direct marketing and be given the right to object free of charge. The Safe Harbor Principles are not as explicit. It is also not clear how behavior tracking services such as DoubleClick fit into the strict definition of onward transfer that was formulated by the EU back in 1995 when web marketing was still in its infancy. Technically speaking, data are not really transferred anywhere since user clickstreams are simply channeled through the DoubleClick site. Such distinctions highlight the difficulties of applying static regulations to the dynamic Internet environment.

Access

The Safe Harbor Principles state that "individuals must have [reasonable] access to personal information." The directive is more forceful, stating that individuals have the right to access their personal information to verify its accuracy and integrity. U.S. policy does not emphasize access to personal information because of the costs involved in mandating such access for every type of data. As a result, it is fairly unusual for an individual to obtain access to any substantive information files that are being stored on web servers.

Enforcement

The European directive clearly states that a government regulation board must be set up by each of the member states to administer and enforce privacy policies. U.S. policy does not establish any government entity but states that organizations collecting personal data should inform individuals of their methods of recourse if they feel their privacy has been invaded. The U.S. policy dictates that organizations collecting personal information should explain how an individual's complaints and disputes can be investigated and resolved, provide follow-up procedures for verifying business's privacy practices, and define the extent to which the company will be obligated to remedy problems of compliance identified by the individual. U.S. reliance on self-regulation and self-reporting by business as the first and preferred means of enforcement has been cited by the EU as evidence that the United States lacks adequate protection.

In comparing the two approaches to regulation, we see a great deal more overlap on fundamental principles and fewer critical differences in implementation than much of the publicity around the directive would imply. If the EU review of U.S. compliance efforts focused on the information and choice aspects of Internet privacy, rather than emphasizing an immediate requirement for government-backed enforcement, the decision about adequate protection could easily be positive. It is, however, impossible to predict when and if that will happen. Whether or not the EU gives its seal of approval to U.S. practice, an important remaining question is how well those practices are currently working to improve privacy protection on U.S. web sites. That question will be the focus of the final section of this chapter.

Self-Regulation in the United States

In July 1999, the Online Privacy Alliance (OPA), a coalition of industry groups, sent letters to about a hundred U.S. companies from the Media Metrix Top 500 web sites that did not have easy-to-find privacy policies posted on-line. The letters encourage compliance with the following OPA guidelines for privacy policy:

- Be easy to find, read, and understand

- Provide consumers with information about what information is being collected and how it will be used

- Provide information on how to exercise choice

- Disclose the security measures taken to assure the data's reliability

- Provide a contact person with whom to communicate problems or concerns

- Explain the mechanism to provide access to information to assure its accuracy.

Consensus about model privacy protection practices, active private sector leadership, and government support for industry initiatives are essential components for the success of self-regulation, and the United States has a positive track record in these areas. Other important factors include broad participation, buy-in by a significant number of companies, and increased confidence on the part of consumers. In these last two areas, as the recent Federal Trade Commission (FTC) report somewhat euphemistically concludes, "effective self-regulation had not yet taken hold."[13]

One measure of the effectiveness of self-regulation is the percentage of companies that have voluntarily implemented the recommended privacy protection guidelines. In its June 1998 report, *Privacy Online: A Report to Congress*, the Federal Trade Commission detailed the results of a survey of the privacy practices at 1,400 commercial web sites in the United States. At the time of the survey 92 percent of the sites in the sample collected personal information from consumers; but only 14 percent of them posted any disclosure about their information practices, and a mere 2 percent provided a comprehensive privacy policy. Special concern was directed to the finding that 89 percent of the sites designed for children collected personal information; only 24 percent of these posted privacy policies, and only 1 percent required parental consent prior to the collection or disclosure of children's information.

A follow-up study conducted by Georgetown University in March 1999, the Georgetown Internet Privacy Policy Survey (GIPPS), selected a different sample group of 361 web sites. The OPA also commissioned Professor Mary Culnan at Georgetown to conduct a survey of the hundred most visited web sites in the United States. The results of both of these studies are summarized in table 2.

13. Federal Trade Commission, *Self-Regulation and Privacy Online: A Report to Congress*, July 1999, p. 1.

TABLE 2

Summary of Georgetown Internet Privacy Policy Survey (GIPPS)
and Online Privacy Alliance (OPA) Studies

	1999 GIPPS Report	1999 OPA Study
Number of sites in sample	361	100
Number of sites collecting personal information	337	99
Percent of sites in sample collecting personal information	93%	99%
Number of sites posting any privacy disclosure	238	93
Percent of sites in sample posting any privacy disclosure	66%	93%
Number of sites posting policy notice	157	81
Percent of sites in sample posting a privacy policy notice	44%	81%
Number of sites posting a disclosure for all four substantive fair information practice principles	36	22
Percent of sites in sample posting a disclosure for all four substantive fair information practice principles	10%	22%

SOURCE: http:/www.gsb.georgetown.edu/faculty/culnanm/gippshome.html.

After receiving a report of the GIPPS results and reviewing the activities of industry groups to promote voluntary compliance with the fair information practice principles, the Federal Trade Commission concluded in its July 1999 report to Congress that self-regulation was working. There was enough progress to warrant continued reliance on self-regulation accompanied by more of an emphasis on consumer education and support for voluntary compliance efforts such as web seal programs. "Based on these facts, the Commission believes that legislation to address online privacy is not appropriate at this time. We also believe that industry faces some substantial challenges. Specifically, the present challenge is to educate those companies which still do not understand the importance of consumer privacy and to create incentives for further progress toward effective, widespread implementation."[14]

One of the positive steps toward self-regulation highlighted by the FTC has been industry groups' efforts to educate corporations and to encourage them to publicize their compliance with privacy guidelines by participating in one of the recognized privacy seal programs. The FTC report made special mention of the following seal programs as evidence that companies were moving from simply posting privacy statements to a more comprehensive compliance with fair information practices, including a willingness to agree to regular outside reviews.

TRUSTe

TRUSTe is an independent, nonprofit organization founded by the CommerceNet Consortium and the Electronic Frontier Foundation. The TRUSTe program includes third-party monitoring and periodic reviews of licensees' information practices to ensure compliance with program requirements. In "Web Site reviews," TRUSTe examines and monitors changes in licensees' privacy statements and tracks unique identifiers in licensees' databases (a practice known as "seeding") to determine whether consumers' requests to be removed from those databases are being honored. In "On-Site reviews," a third-party auditing firm can be called in, should TRUSTe have reason to believe that a licensee is not in compliance with the terms of the license agreement. Licensees must provide consumers with a way to submit concerns regarding their information practices, and agree to respond to all reasonable inquiries within five days.

TRUSTe also plays a part in resolving consumer complaints. When there's a problem, it could surface either through TRUSTe's auditing or via a consumer complaint. First, TRUSTe sends off a formal notice and gives the target an opportunity to respond. If the response is inadequate, TRUSTe can pursue it according to contract—revoking the license and the mark, auditing the miscre-

14. Ibid., p. 2.

ant (at the licensee's cost), and publicizing the results. If the breach appears willful and fraudulent, TRUSTe can call in the local jurisdiction under which the license was signed (usually a U.S. court) and sue. TRUSTe can also call in the FTC or other government agencies in serious cases. TRUSTe provides for public reporting of complaints and, in appropriate circumstances, will refer complaints to the Federal Trade Commission.[15]

BBB*Online*

BBB*Online*, a subsidiary of the Council of Better Business Bureaus, launched its privacy seal program for on-line businesses on March 17, 1999. In order to be awarded the BBB*Online* Privacy Seal, applicants must post a privacy policy that comports with the program's information practice principles, complete a "Compliance Assessment Questionnaire," and agree to participate in a consumer dispute resolution system and to submit to monitoring and review by BBB*Online*.

The BBB*Online* Privacy Seal Program covers "individually identifiable information," as well as "prospect information," which is identifying retrievable information that is collected by the company's web site from one individual about another. The BBB*Online* Privacy Seal Program's consumer complaint resolution procedure is bolstered by several compliance incentives, including public reporting of decisions, suspension or revocation of the BBB*Online* seal, or referral to federal agencies, as sanctions for noncompliance. BBB*Online* has committed to adopting a third-party verification system, although this aspect of the program has not yet been implemented.[16]

Despite the FTC's plaudits for these and other industry-specific trusted seal groups, the penetration rate of voluntary seal programs is still minuscule. In January 2000, TRUSTe announced the award of its one thousandth privacy seal. According to a recent OCLC

15. From the TRUSTe web site, www.truste.org.
16. From the BBB*Online* web site, www.bbbonline.org.

study, approximately 2.2 million public web sites provide substantive content on the Internet.[17] Given the high percentage of sample sites that are collecting some form of personal information, well more than a million sites must still be recruited to voluntary privacy protection programs. Is there any realistic outlook that the majority of these sites will actively support fair information practices?

There are a few positive indicators. Voluntary posting of existing privacy policies is already the most common privacy feature of U.S. web sites according to the Georgetown survey, and it is spreading quickly. Developing a statement to describe what a web site does with the information it collects is not particularly burdensome. TRUSTe among others provides sample statements and even offers a privacy policy wizard to simplify the process of creating a customized statement. If corporations that advocate published privacy policies all begin to require their suppliers, marketing, and business partners to display their privacy practices on the web, the adoption rate will accelerate.

Providing web visitors with an easy-to-exercise choice to opt out of certain data collection practices is more challenging. Some companies may find themselves with significantly less valuable databases of customer information if a high percentage of their visitors opt out of participation, to the detriment of their revenue issues and business models. But concern about turning off customers would put a premium on appropriate incentives to convince visitors to opt in to the data collection. In the long run, the need to provide positive customer motivation to share information would create more loyal customers. Aside from the business issues it may

---

17. Online Computer Library Center (OCLC), Inc. OCLC Research Report, *Web Characterization Project*, "June 1999 Statistics," www.oclc.org/research/projects/webstats/statistics.htm.

pose, providing choice to web visitors is becoming more feasible even for smaller companies. The W3 Consortium, an organization devoted to developing Internet standards and interoperability tools, has published a standard called P3P to facilitate consumers' ability to express their privacy preferences on any web site. The availability of the P3P standard from the W3 Consortium and the development of related, efficient tools make offering visitors an easy-to-navigate data collection choice a realistic component for any web site.

If the majority of U.S. web sites provided a clear statement about their privacy practices—and abided by it consistently—that would be an important first step. If those same sites offered their visitors a clear means to exercise control over the use of their personal data, that would go a long way toward addressing some of the fundamental privacy protection and consumer confidence issues discussed in this chapter.

Adoption and publication of a voluntary code of practice by corporate web sites are only part of the change that is needed for self-regulation to become a real force for protecting on-line privacy. Another important factor is an educated and proactive public. It is essential for individual Internet users to take more active responsibility for demanding and exercising the right to choose when and how to share information with web sites. Without any indication of a significant user demand for privacy at the point of on-line interaction, the motivation for companies to adhere to voluntary policies will be considerably less. Although a majority of consumers sampled in surveys express concern about privacy in the abstract, the actual behavior of on-line users today would seem to support the argument that the average consumer is quite willing to share a great deal of information in exchange for on-line convenience and customization. Web site owners will understandably attach more significance to what the visitors to their home page actually do on-line than to survey reports about general privacy concerns.

One indication that industry leaders are interested in increasing public awareness is the privacy education campaign announced by NetCoaltion.com in November 1999. NetCoalition is a public policy organization founded by leading Internet companies including Amazon.com, eBay, DoubleClick, *Excite@Home*, Inktomi, Lycos, theglobe.com, and Yahoo! These companies account for a sizable percentage of total on-line web visits. By espousing good privacy practice as a central organizational mission and dedicating a portion of the huge on-line resources of its member sites to educational messages about privacy, NetCoalition will at least raise public awareness of good privacy practice. Whether this will translate into more user initiatives to protect personal information remains to be seen.

The privacy scorecard received some negative marks in the fall of 1999 with a number of unexpected revelations about personal data collection practices and on-line profiling tools that were operating on popular web sites without clear disclosure to users. Richard Smith, a privacy and security consultant, published a report on his personal web site on October 31, 1999, detailing user information monitoring and reporting features of the free Real-Jukebox software that RealNetworks provides to play MP3 files on the desktop. Smith noted:

> I quickly discovered that the RealJukeBox software is sending off information to RealNetworks about what music CDs I listen to, along with a unique player ID number that identifies who I am. I also found that the RealJukeBox sends back to RealNetworks, on a daily basis, information on how I am using the product. It reports things like how many songs I have recorded on my hard drive, the type of portable MP3 player I own, and my music preferences.[18]

18. Richard Smith, personal web site, www.tiac.net/users/smiths/privacy.

More than twelve million users had downloaded and installed RealJukeBox on their desktops since its release in the summer of 1999, so this secret monitoring capability was generating a huge file of personal music preferences and listening habits for Real-Networks to harvest. By linking the e-mail address collected as part of the software registration process with the unique identifying number on the software, the company was also in a position to track individuals by name rather than just aggregate the data for market research purposes. None of the capabilities built into the RealJukeBox software and deployed on individual desktops was disclosed in the privacy policy that was displayed on the Real-Networks web site.

RealNetworks moved quickly to try to control the potential repercussions Smith's report might have on its relationships with customers. The company issued a software patch that would disable the RealJukeBox's ability to send daily reports of music listening habits back to RealNetwork's server. Rob Glaser, chairman and CEO of RealNetworks, issued a statement on November 1 that said in part, "We made a mistake in not being clear enough to our users about what kinds of data was being generated and transmitted by the use of RealJukebox. We respect and value the privacy of our users, and we deeply apologize for doing anything that suggests otherwise."[19] The company also promised to review all of its data collection practices in consultation with outside privacy experts to ensure that it was fully compliant with recommended privacy policies and to lay out more consistent privacy protection guidelines for any future collection and use of customer data.

Additional information about how other large companies are tracking on-line behavior without explicit consumer consent emerged as a result of a public hearing in November 1999. This

---

19. Posted on the RealNetworks web site on November 1, 1999, www.real.com.

hearing, jointly sponsored by the Federal Trade Commission and the Department of Commerce, focused on current practices of on-line profiling. In inviting comments, the agencies acknowledged that this aspect of Internet data collection was increasingly prevalent and particularly difficult for users to exercise opt-out choices. "Consumers are largely unaware of the creation of online profiles, and the implementation of core fair information practices of notice, choice, access and security with respect to the collection of information in online profiles remains a significant challenge."[20]

Testimony at the hearing from Richard Smith highlighted yet another undisclosed on-line monitoring technique being used by many popular web sites without any disclosure to their users. Dubbed *web bugs* or *clear GIFs* these small files are included on web pages or in e-mail messages to keep track of who is browsing the page or reading the e-mail. According to Smith, companies using this tracking technology include Quicken, Federal Express, Barnes and Noble, eToys, and Microsoft. Uses for these web bugs include finding if and when a particular e-mail message has been read, keeping track of the number of unique visitors to a web site, and linking a record of the visit to any previously set profiles for that individual. These uses may not be disturbing to most Internet users, but they are clearly part of the information-gathering strategy of any web site that uses them, and they can be linked to individual users. Yet Smith noted that none of the web sites where he found web bugs at work made any mention of their existence or functionality in their privacy disclosure statements.

The persistence of unreported web-tracking mechanisms raises a number of questions about the effectiveness of self-regulation in the absence of a well-informed, technically savvy, and vigilant watchdog representing the public interest. Even more sobering for

20. Department of Commerce and Federal Trade Commission, Docket No. 990811219-9219-01, Public Workshop on Online Profiling.

the supporters of self-regulation, the backlash aroused by repeated reports of on-line privacy violations creates a sense among consumers that mandated protections may be the safest course of action. It seems clear that the details of on-line profiling are complex enough and the practice invisible enough that most Internet users would never uncover them. Public education campaigns may encourage users to exercise opt-out opportunities and to read the posted privacy policy statements on their favorite web sites, but they won't make the average on-line shopper an expert on cookies, clear GIFs, and other tracking tools. If on-line companies don't disclose the use of such software in clear, nontechnical terms, then consumers will be misled and most likely feel put upon when they do read reports of such practices in the popular media. When the well-known and respected companies fail to comply with the spirit as well as the letter of good privacy practice, the disillusionment is magnified.

In the context of repeated revelations about behind-the-scenes data gathering in the fall of 1999, it is perhaps no surprise that Forrester Research reports that the majority of consumers it has surveyed are ready to propose a ban on any sale of on-line data to third parties and that half are leaning toward government regulation:

> Forrester found that on-line shoppers are most concerned abut how much personal information they give and who sees it. Web users worry that the information they share online will produce unsolicited spam or telemarketing calls. As a result, 80% of Internet users support a policy that prohibits the sale of data to third parties, and half of online customers are willing to contact the government to regulate online privacy.[21]

---

21. Forrester Research, "The Privacy Best Practice," October 1999, www.forrester.com.

Who Do You Trust?

Companies intent on deploying the full arsenal of tracking software and on-line profiling tools in the interest of more effective interactive marketing are veering dangerously close to killing off the goose—in this case, the unsuspecting public—that is providing them with golden nuggets of information. Collecting information about any user's on-line behavior in secret, without proper advance notice and explanations, puts future relationships at risk. This tactic may generate reams of data on preference patterns and response rates, but it is the opposite of building a trusted relationship with an individual customer. In the long run, the web site that earns the most user trust will be in the best position to maintain customer loyalty, not the companies that rely on stealth personalization to customize their advertising and offers.

Even in the short term, stealth personalization is likely to backfire because the net is populated with technically sophisticated users such as Richard Smith who are willing to devote considerable time to researching and reporting on the dubious on-line practices of large companies. It is almost impossible to keep on-line profiling and other data-gathering activity on a web site secret from someone who is determined to ferret it out. The media is also always ready to report on the latest Internet exposé. Although it is true that revelations about privacy violations have not yet triggered a consumer stampede to privacy protection and data collection blocking options such as enonymous.com, these alternatives are growing in number and are attracting a following. Once an individual signs up with such a service, his or her data are effectively lost to the average web merchant. The Internet has given consumers unprecedented choice and comparative shopping power, and they are gradually learning to exercise this power in their own best interests.

What makes covert data collection tactics all the more counterproductive is the fact that many on-line users would happily share a great deal more information than is now being gathered, and do it more directly, if they had a sense of trust in the requestor and a clear choice about how that information was going to be used. Web sites can offer users a variety of incentives to stimulate positive opt-ins and consent to on-line profiling. Many consumers would be likely to consent to sharing personal data with third parties, as long as they clearly understand how they will benefit from it and are informed in advance about its collection. Ample evidence from other media, such as talk radio and daytime television, indicates that U.S. consumers will reveal most anything about themselves given the right incentives. In addition, the willingness to share personal information within a community context has always been a characteristic of the Internet. The number of discussion lists, interactive boards, and on-line chat groups dedicated to personal topics is ample testimony to this tendency. Any number of private acts, from sex to childbirth to psychological counseling, have found a home and an audience on the public web. The difference between these self-revelations and the unreported data collection that takes place on many web sites is the element of individual choice and control.

There is every reason to believe that cultural norms around privacy for Internet users in general and for U.S. users in particular are elastic enough to accommodate a vast level of information collection and analysis and that this willingness to share information in exchange for value will expand with time. But continued revelations that companies with respected reputations are tracking their customers in secret could reverse this natural trend and make privacy protection a political cause. Web sites caught collecting marketing-driven and basically benign information intended to improve on-line personalization may well be equated rhetorically with a "big brother" invasion of all individual privacy rights.

Push the new group of on-line consumers into information disclosure without their knowledge and consent, and there may well be a backlash that would set back consumer trust and the personalization potential of the net to the detriment of all. Analysis of the current EU regulations demonstrates that this is far from impossible. The burden rests with the information-dependent on-line companies to show that their data collection flow is coming from well-informed consumers who have agreed to participate in its creation and who know that they have the ultimate choice of where to entrust their personal information on the net. The company that can give consumers the most value in exchange for personal data will earn their trust and will be able to build a stronger relationship on that open information exchange

Conclusion

We are just coming to terms with the full ramifications of implementing appropriate standards for on-line privacy protection. It is still too early to anoint a single model as the best way to ensure privacy best practices or to regard the persistence of dubious on-line tracking and data collection practices as proof positive that voluntary corporate compliance can never work. Like many other Internet phenomena, privacy issues seem destined to become a permanent work in progress. There are, however, some lessons that we should draw from the privacy debate thus far and some common goals that should unite the efforts of responsible corporate citizens, privacy advocates, and individual consumers.

In framing the next stage of discussion about on-line privacy, we need to focus more on the positive value that enhanced choice and user control will generate for on-line companies. Unless there is a clear case for the business benefits of good privacy practices, it will be an uphill battle to convince small and medium-size companies to incur expenses and forgo potential revenues in order to comply with voluntary standards. The threat of government intervention or European Union prosecution or expressions of consumer concern may be a powerful short-term stick, but it will not prevail against economic self-interest.

One problem with the current emphasis on on-line privacy protection is that, like security, it focuses on preventing bad things from happening. That is a necessary but self-limiting precondition for the growth of electronic commerce. Good privacy practice should be more closely linked with trust, as an essential building block for closer relationships with customers and a sustainable source of eBusiness advantage. To the extent that on-line companies conceal their data collection practices from consumers, they are forfeiting the opportunity to earn and consolidate that trust. At the most obvious level, they are risking disastrous damage to their reputation if and when hidden customer monitoring and tracking practices are revealed. Even more profoundly, they are failing to use the full power of the Internet as a two-way communication channel that empowers the consumer to express preferences directly as well as implicitly. If we are serious about getting millions of on-line companies to practice what self-regulation advocates preach, then it's time to link privacy and trust more closely.

What does this mean for the policy questions posed at the outset of the chapter? On the basis of the on-line privacy track record in the United States to date, some specific recommendations are indicated:

- For the next three years at least, there is a need for a regular and independent external review body to advocate for model on-line privacy practices and to monitor the performance of heavily trafficked web sites in complying with these model practices on a regular basis.

- This external review need not be based on formal government regulations. Existing industry organizations such as TRUSTe, combined with the efforts of privacy advocacy groups and individual watchdogs, could expand their efforts sufficiently to fulfill this function as long as there is support from the appropriate government agencies such as the Federal Trade Commission.

- Consumer understanding of and involvement in evaluating web privacy practices and demanding improvement where necessary is well below the level required for market controls to have any significant impact on merchant behavior on the web. Voluntary campaigns such as the NetCoalition privacy program are a good start but not enough. This is an area where more direct public and private sector leadership is essential.

- Lapses in on-line privacy practice at popular web sites are likely to be uncovered with some regularity over the next several years, as companies test the boundaries of consumer sensitivities and commercial self-interest. It is essential for self-regulatory groups to take a strong stance when privacy violations are discovered.

The most enduring drivers of Internet growth and diversity have been the net's openness to all comers and its insistence on network participants' abiding by a consistent set of cooperatively developed technical standards. The standards for respecting the privacy of individual Internet users are far from universally accepted and practiced by companies on the web today. Given the size and heterogeneity of the on-line merchant community, it is unrealistic to expect universal compliance with any code of on-line conduct, whether voluntary or legally binding. There is no shortcut to perfect privacy on the Internet, and reliance on legislation would trigger more problems than it would solve.

A recommendation against on-line privacy legislation does not, however, constitute an endorsement of the status quo for personal data collection on the web. It is essential for the United States to achieve a better balance between the interests of corporate web sites in collecting valuable consumer information and the interests of individuals in having the final say about their personal data and who has access to that information. The key to that balance will be expanded cooperative efforts on the part of consumers, advocacy groups, government agencies, and corporate leaders to articulate and enforce responsible web privacy practices. It will take time and constant vigilance, but it is worth the effort.

Charles E. McLure Jr.

2   The Taxation of Electronic Commerce: Background and Proposal

The rise of electronic commerce raises fundamental questions of tax policy. Most fundamentally, should electronic commerce be taxed? Is the answer the same in the short run as in the long run? How about arguments that electronic commerce should not be taxed during its infancy? How would the exemption of electronic commerce affect Main Street merchants? What are the implications for tax revenues of exempting electronic commerce? for the distribution of income?

If electronic commerce is to be taxed, how should it be done? Can electronic commerce actually be taxed as it should be? What are the technological, legal, and political impediments? What simplifications of tax laws and administration are required to tax electronic commerce? Are there "technological fixes" for the problems?

If electronic commerce should not be taxed, what technique should be used to effect the exemption? How is electronic commerce defined? How can the benefits of an exemption be limited to the intended beneficiaries?

There are also questions of relationships between governments. What are the implications for fiscal federalism of exempting electronic commerce? for international fiscal relations?

This chapter provides background for a discussion of these and other issues and summarizes some of my views. Although the chapter touches on questions of international income taxation, it focuses primarily on the state sales and use tax. (Use tax is levied on the purchaser's use of a taxed good in the taxing state; it is intended to compensate for the constitutional prohibition against requiring vendors to charge sales tax on interstate sales.) Most of the first part of the chapter provides a neutral survey of issues, but it also expresses my personal view that electronic commerce should not be permanently exempt from sales and use tax. The second part reproduces the proposal I presented to the Advisory Commission on Electronic Commerce (ACEC) in December 1999. It indicates how I think the issues raised in the first part of the chapter should be resolved. The third part—a concluding commentary on the application of state sales and use tax to electronic commerce—ends by challenging state and local governments to simplify those taxes, so that collecting them would not unduly burden electronic commerce.

Survey of Issues

Electronic commerce can usefully be defined as "the use of computer networks to facilitate transactions involving the production, distribution, and sale and delivery of goods and services in the marketplace."[1]

This chapter discusses three types of electronic commerce:

- Commerce in *tangible products* (e.g., books, computers, and wine)

- Commerce in *digitized content* downloaded from the Internet (e.g., software, music, games, and videos)

- *Internet access*, which is usefully discussed with telecommunications, for reasons explained below

The chapter does not consider the taxation of travel or of financial services, among the largest components of electronic commerce, because the issues encountered in these industries are unique to them.

For purposes of definition, remote sales are transactions that cross state or national boundaries and thus raise questions of the constitutional taxing powers of the states and of international relations in the tax field. For most purposes, traditional remote commerce means mail order, but it also includes sales made across the counter for shipment to another state, as well as telemarketing and TV shopping. Electronic commerce is a nontraditional form of remote sale.

---

1. Howard E. Abrams and Richard L. Doernberg, "How Electronic Commerce Works," *State Tax Notes* 13 (May 1997): 123–36. I find this definition more useful, if slightly less accurate, than the one in Organisation for Economic Co-operation and Development, *The Economic and Social Impact of Electronic Commerce: Preliminary Findings and Research Agenda* (Paris: OECD, 1999), p. 28: "business occurring over networks which use non-proprietary protocols that are established through an open standard setting process such as the Internet."

Arguments for and against Preferential Taxation of Electronic Commerce

Some believe fervently that, as a matter of principle, electronic commerce should not be taxed; others strongly believe that it should be.[2]

FOR PREFERENTIAL TAX TREATMENT

Although arguments for preferential tax treatment of electronic commerce are not always well specified, one encounters the following. Fear that a "bit tax" might be imposed on every bit of information transmitted over the Internet—and that a variety of other novel taxes might be targeted at the Internet—gave rise to the cry of "no new taxes" on the Internet.[3] Logically implicit in this view, but rarely explicit, is that existing taxes can and should be applied to electronic commerce.

Some, making an "infant industry" argument, favor no taxes whatsoever on the Internet, justifying preferential treatment as a way to stimulate development of electronic commerce.[4] They suggest that taxing electronic commerce would throw sand in the gears of economic progress. To support their position they cite studies

2. For further discussion, see Charles E. McLure Jr., "Electronic Commerce and the State Retail Sales Tax: A Challenge to American Federalism," *International Tax and Public Finance* 6 (May 1999): 193–224.

3. For the proposal of a bit tax, see Arthur J. Cordell, "Multijurisdictional Taxation of Electronic Commerce," and Luc Soete, "Taxing Consumption in the Electronic Age: The European Bit Tax Proposal," both presented at the symposium on Multi-Jurisdictional Taxation of Electronic Commerce, Harvard Law School, Cambridge, Mass., April 5, 1997. Although the bit tax might seem to have died quickly and quietly, the United Nations Development Programme has proposed a bit tax to help provide telephone and Internet service in poor nations. Congressman Chris Cox maintains a list of "Internet tax horror stories" on his "Internet Tax Freedom Act" web site, www.house.gov/cox/nettax/.

4. See James S. Gilmore III, "No Internet Tax: A Proposal Submitted to the 'Policies & Options' Paper of the Advisory Commission on Electronic Commerce," available at www.ecommercecommission.org.

by Austan Goolsbee of the University of Chicago reporting on the importance of network externalities and the negative effects taxation has on electronic commerce.[5] They generally do not specify whether preferential treatment is to be temporary or permanent, although Goolsbee clearly advocates at most a temporary moratorium on taxation of electronic commerce.[6]

Still others stress that, to the extent electronic commerce involves interstate trade, it would be protected from the duty to collect use tax under the U.S. Supreme Court decision in *Quill* (described and discussed below). This view neglects to mention that the Court indicated clearly that Congress has the constitutional power to override this decision.

Finally, some take a "feet-to-the fire" approach, arguing that if electronic commerce is tax free, local merchants will be more likely to pressure their legislatures and governors to keep taxes down.[7] This is a special case of the theory being espoused by many conservatives that "a good tax is a bad tax and a bad tax is a good tax."

---

5. Austan Goolsbee, "In a World without Borders: The Impact of Taxes on Internet Commerce," forthcoming, *Quarterly Journal of Economics*; Austan Goolsbee and Jonathan Zittrain, "Evaluating the Costs and Benefits of Taxing Internet Commerce," *National Tax Journal* 52, no. 3 (September 1999): 413–28; and Austan Goolsbee and Peter Klenow, "Evidence on Learning and Network Externalities in the Diffusion of Home Computers," National Bureau of Economic Research, Working Paper No. 7329, September 1999.

6. Goolsbee and Zittrain, "Evaluating the Costs and Benefits of Taxing Internet Commerce," p. 424, state that "the major network externalities are likely to exhaust or at least diminish once the Internet achieves major scale. Too often, infant industry protection turns into established industry protection. Further, we expect that eventually there will be an important negative network externality . . . increasing Internet congestion. . . . The congestion problem is likely to get worse as the Internet grows and it argues against subsidizing the growth rate through tax policies." Goolsbee signed the "Appeal for Fair and Equal Taxation of Electronic Commerce" presented to the Advisory Commission on Electronic Commerce on December 15, 1999, and reproduced in the appendix to this chapter.

7. Both Milton Friedman and Grover Norquist, a member of the ACEC, have made this argument in personal conversation with the author.

In that view it would be a mistake to reform the sales tax to conform more closely to the conceptual ideal or to make it simpler; the
worse the tax, the more pain it inflicts and the more difficult it is to
finance big government. One problem with that view is that the
taxation of business inputs under the present arrangements results
in a substantial hidden tax burden. It is estimated that as much as
40 percent of sales tax revenues come from sales to business.[8]

AGAINST PREFERENTIAL TAX TREATMENT

Opponents of preferential treatment of electronic commerce
generally agree that there should be no *new* taxes on the Internet
and no taxes that discriminate against electronic commerce but
that electronic commerce should be taxed like other commerce.
They oppose preferential treatment on several grounds.

First, they argue that, by substituting the judgment of politi-
cians, bureaucrats, and industry spokespersons for that of the market, preferential treatment of electronic commerce would distort
economic decision making and create economic inefficiency, as tax
advantages may cause more costly e-commerce alternatives to be
chosen over traditional forms of commerce. They acknowledge,
without regret, that electronic commerce may supplant traditional
commerce in some sectors because of its convenience. They do not,
however, want to see traditional commerce shackled by the need
to collect sales tax and electronic commerce not being required to
collect use tax. To them the Goolsbee analysis provides evidence of
the economic distortion that would be created by not taxing electronic commerce while taxing competing activities. By supporting
the "Appeal for Fair and Equal Taxation of Electronic Commerce," which was presented to the ACEC on December 15, 1999

---

8. See Raymond J. Ring Jr., "Consumers' Share and Producers' Share in the
General Sales Tax," *National Tax Journal* 52 (March 1999): 79–90.

(and reproduced as an appendix to this chapter), more than 170 academic tax specialists, most of them economists, and two winners of the Nobel Prize in economics (Kenneth Arrow and James Tobin) have opposed a permanent exemption for electronic commerce.

Second, those who argue against preferential treatment claim it would be unfair. It would widen the "digital divide," favoring those who are computer literate and who have access to computers—and to the telephone lines and credit cards needed for Internet access—almost certainly the more affluent members of society.[9] Perhaps worse, it would place Main Street merchants at a competitive disadvantage relative to vendors in electronic commerce. By comparison, equal treatment of electronic and nonelectronic commerce would create a level playing field.

Third, opponents argue that preferential treatment of electronic commerce is not needed—that the growth of electronic commerce is not likely to be seriously hampered by taxation that creates a level playing field. They note the explosive growth of electronic commerce and the easy access to capital enjoyed by Internet ventures. More generally, they doubt the validity of "infant industry" arguments for preferential tax treatment.

Fourth, they note that there will be an increasingly important negative effect on revenues of state and local governments if electronic commerce is not taxed. The reduction in revenues will be especially dramatic if intrastate electronic commerce is exempt because all commerce will become electronic in form. Fifth, they doubt that, once granted on "infant industry" grounds, preferential treatment of electronic commerce could easily be withdrawn.

---

9. On the digital divide, see U.S. Department of Commerce, National Telecommunications and Information Administration, "Falling through the Net: Defining the Digital Divide" (1999).

Impediments to Equal Tax Treatment of Electronic Commerce

Even if it were agreed that electronic commerce and nonelectronic commerce should be taxed alike, there are impediments.

TECHNOLOGICAL/ADMINISTRATIVE CONSTRAINTS

A cartoon pictures two dogs sitting in front of a computer screen. One says to the other, "On the Internet, no one knows you are a dog." This truth has fundamental implications for the implementation of tax policy, especially by market jurisdictions.

Tax administrators may not know the identity, or even the location, of the parties to a transaction conducted over the Internet. Indeed, vendors may not know the identity or location of their customers. The anonymity of Internet transactions seriously complicates both tax administration and tax compliance, if taxes are based on the destination of sales or the source of income.

Unlike tangible products, digital content does not stop at the border, the customs house, or the post office and cannot be made to do so, at least with present technology. (Whereas both tangible and digitized products can be ordered on-line, only digitized content can be delivered on-line.) Moreover, since digital content can be reproduced without cost and is not warehoused, it is not possible to check production records or inventories to see how much has been sold.

Vendors of digitized content may be located in foreign countries (including countries not a party to tax treaties) and thus beyond the reach of tax authorities. Finally, payment for purchases in electronic commerce may be made with digital money that cannot be traced or with credit cards issued by financial institutions in countries with strict bank secrecy laws. (Digital money would be a credit balance purchased from a financial institution or other issuer; it would be especially useful to pay for small transactions, such as games or single plays of digitized music. It might be stored on "smart cards" similar to prepaid phone cards that could be read by a computer or it might be transferred directly to a computer.) Where these four attributes (anonymity, digital content, foreign vendor, and untraceable money) are found together, effective tax administration may be almost impossible.

LEGAL CONSTRAINTS

Laws specifying the taxation of electronic commerce are not being written on a clean slate; rather, they are being considered in the context of existing laws, agreements, and practices.

The State Sales and Use Tax. Application of state sales and use tax to electronic commerce must be considered in the light of the decision of the U.S. Supreme Court in *Quill*[10] that effectively exempts many remote sales of tangible products. Under the *Quill* decision, remote vendors cannot be required to collect use tax unless they have a physical presence in the state. (A physical presence is said to constitute *nexus.* The state of North Dakota had argued that Quill, a major mail order house, had an economic presence in the state that justified the state's requirement that it collect use tax on sales made to customers in the state. The Court's reasoning is described below.) This case law may be applied to electronic commerce, including that in digital content. Moreover, efforts to achieve a level playing field for electronic commerce must consider the preferential tax treatment of other remote sales with which electronic commerce competes. If it is impossible to alter the current de facto tax exemption of other remote sales, the optimal tax treatment of electronic commerce is not obvious.

International Income Tax Rules. National laws of various

---

10. *Quill Corp. V. North Dakota*, 504 U.S. 298 (1992). For a masterful analysis of *Quill*, see Walter Hellerstein, "Supreme Court Says No State Use Tax Imposed on Mail-Order Sellers . . . for Now," *Journal of Taxation* 77 (August 1992): 120–24.

countries contain provisions that, absent modification, will control the taxation of income from electronic commerce.[11] The "rules of the game" for the taxation of income from international economic relations are found primarily in bilateral treaties, especially between developed countries. These, in turn, are commonly based on the Model Treaty of the Organisation for Economic Co-operation and Development (OECD). National laws and treaties were not written with electronic commerce in mind and thus do not easily accommodate it. Changing domestic legislation and renegotiating treaties are time-consuming activities with uncertain outcomes.

POLITICAL CONSTRAINTS

Efforts to apply sales tax to electronic commerce or to apply income tax to it in ways that deviate from present practice would encounter political opposition.

Overriding Quill.   In principle, the U.S. Congress, acting under the power granted by the Constitution to regulate interstate commerce, could enact legislation to override the *Quill* decision, substituting a less demanding test for the physical presence test of nexus. This would be difficult because of the political power of the direct marketing industry, which can mobilize letter-writing campaigns by thousands of customers. The direct marketers have now been joined by those engaged in electronic commerce, which seems to enjoy support based on a special mystique. Of course, political power is not found only on one side, but those favoring equal taxation—largely government officials and a few academics to date, but increasingly Main Street merchants—appear thus far to have less political clout than advocates of exemption.

---

11. This and the subsequent discussion of international aspects of the income taxation of electronic commerce draw on Charles E. McLure Jr., "Taxation of Electronic Commerce: Economic Objectives, Technological Constraints, and Tax Law," *Tax Law Review* 52 (spring 1997): 269–423, and references cited there.

Federalism Aspects.   Some proposed solutions to the "mail order problem," and thus the question of how to tax electronic commerce, involve expanding the duty of remote vendors to collect use tax, in exchange for substantial simplification of sales and use taxes. Among the simplifications that may be required are greater uniformity of state sales tax systems and a single local sales tax rate in a given state.[12] Both elements would be difficult to realize under the American system of fiscal federalism, in which the individual states have substantial fiscal sovereignty and local governments have considerable political power. Congressional action in this area, even if taken only to ratify state initiatives, would represent a worrisome encroachment on the fiscal autonomy of the states.

The Difficulty of Fundamental Reform.   Some believe that this is a unique opportunity to rationalize a defective state sales tax system inherited from the industrial age—that fundamental reform is needed and tinkering will not suffice.[13] In that view, all sales to business should be exempt, virtually all sales to households, whether of goods, services, or intangible products, should be taxed, and sales by remote vendors should be taxed like sales by local merchants. But enormous inertia resists such a change. Moreover, there is no institutional framework for a fundamental and coordinated reform of state taxes.[14] Worse, there is no political constituency for such a reform, but substantial opposition to it.

---

12. See National Tax Association Communications and Electronic Commerce Tax Project, "Final Report," September 1999, available at www.ntanet.org.

13. For the author's view, see Charles E. McLure Jr., "Electronic Commerce and the Tax Assignment Problem: Preserving State Sovereignty in a Digital World," *State Tax Notes* 14 (April 13, 1998): 1169–81, and Charles E. McLure Jr., "Achieving a Level Playing Field for Electronic Commerce" *State Tax Notes* 14 (June 1, 1998): 1767–83, as well as the second part of this chapter.

14. The National Conference of Commissioners on Uniform State Laws might draft a model unified law, but they would do so only in response to a request from the states.

International Aspects. Some changes in the rules of the game for the taxation of income from international economic relations are likely to involve substantial redistribution of tax revenues among countries. For example, the United States has suggested a shift to greater reliance on taxation by the country of residence of firms engaged in electronic commerce.[15] It cannot be expected that countries that would lose revenue will gladly acquiesce in such changes. Unlike the situation in the areas of contracts and intellectual property, where other nations may follow the lead of the United States, in the tax area decisions are more likely to be made on a multilateral basis, especially in the forum provided by the OECD.[16] Other nations will listen to the U.S. position, but they will not be led by the nose.

Norms, Practices, and Proposals: State Sales Taxation

Before examining state practices in the sales tax area and proposals to modify them, it is useful to consider norms against which to judge them.

NORMS FOR TAXATION OF SALES BETWEEN JURISDICTIONS

Economists describe two internally consistent systems for the taxation of sales that cross the borders of political jurisdictions, be they states or nations.[17]

Under the *destination principle*, tax is imposed on imports into the taxing jurisdiction but not on exports (and any amount collected before the export stage is refunded). A destination-based tax is a tax on consumption occurring in the taxing jurisdiction.

---

15. U.S. Department of the Treasury, Office of Tax Policy, "Selected Policy Implications of Global Electronic Commerce," November 1996.

16. For activities of the OECD, see www.oecd.org/daf/fa/e_com/e_com.htm.

17. For further discussion, see McLure, "Taxation of Electronic Commerce," and McLure, "Electronic Commerce and the Tax Assignment Problem."

Under the *origin principle,* tax is imposed on exports from the taxing jurisdiction and imports are not taxed (but tax is collected on value added after the import stage). An origin-based tax is a tax on production in the taxing jurisdiction.

The destination principle is almost universally employed for the sales taxation of international trade in tangible products, and the European Union appears to be moving toward destination-based taxation of intangibles and services. Destination-based taxation has several conceptual advantages. First, destination-based taxation is much less likely to distort the location of economic activity than is origin-based taxation. Second, taxation of consumption is probably a better proxy for the benefits of public services than taxation of production. (For example, people send their children to school where they live and consume, not where they work and produce.)

Perhaps more important is the political attraction of the destination principle. It is hard to imagine that those producing for the domestic market would quietly accept origin-based taxation, as it implies that they pay taxes while their foreign competition does not. Under the destination principle market jurisdictions would collect the same tax on domestic and foreign production. Similarly, exporters are not likely to take kindly to a suggestion that exports should be taxed.

It is relatively easy, ignoring legal obstacles for the moment, to collect destination-based taxes on tangible products. Where there are fiscal borders, as between nations that are not members of a common market, tax can be collected at the border. Within a common market, it may be possible for vendors to collect the tax because they know where they ship goods. Destination-based taxation of digital content transmitted over the Internet is more difficult to implement because of the difficulty of determining the location of purchasers. By comparison, origin-based taxation would be relatively easy to implement. But if applied to electronic commerce in digital content, origin-based taxation might create a "race to the bottom," in which jurisdictions vie to attract footloose firms by exempting electronic commerce.

OVERVIEW OF PRACTICE: STATE SALES AND USE TAX

For the most part, state sales and use taxes follow the destination principle.[18] That is, exports from a state are commonly exempt from sales tax in that state and local vendors collect sales tax on products that are imported, as well as those produced within the state. There are three important exceptions to the generalization that states sales and use taxes are destination based.

First, when a consumer engages in *cross-border shopping*, buying something in another state and bringing it back home for consumption, tax is ordinarily collected where the sale occurs, instead of where the product is consumed. There is no easy remedy for this problem, short of the highly undesirable step of imposing fiscal borders between states.

Second, many *business inputs* are subject to tax, which is not refunded when products are shipped outside the state; this interjects an element of origin-based taxation. Finally, because of *Quill* remote sales to households are commonly not subject to tax unless the vendor has a physical presence in the market state.

The last point implies that demands for "technologically neutral" taxation of electronic commerce are doomed to failure. Neutrality cannot be achieved relative to both Main Street merchants, who generally collect tax on sales of tangible products, and other remote vendors, who commonly do not collect use tax on sales to households.[19]

18. The standard reference is John F. Due and John L. Mikesell, *Sales Taxation: State and Local Structure and Administration*, 2d ed. (Washington, D.C.: Urban Institute Press, 1994).
19. This point is developed in greater detail in McLure, "Taxation of Electronic Commerce."

DE FACTO EXEMPTION OF REMOTE SALES TO HOUSEHOLDS

The preferential tax treatment of remote sales deserves elaboration because of its importance in the debate on the taxation of electronic commerce. Here, in a nutshell, is the constitutional state of affairs, as determined by decisions of the U.S. Supreme Court.[20]

States cannot apply their *sales tax* to sales made by remote vendors because title passes (or can be made to pass) outside the state. State can levy *use tax* on the use of a product in the state, but the use tax must be levied on the user, not the vendor. Use tax cannot realistically be collected unless (a) the product is registered to be used in the state, (b) the purchaser is a business that is subject to audit in the state, or (c) the vendor can be required to collect the tax. It is generally not cost-effective to attempt to collect use tax directly from nonbusiness purchasers. But under *Quill* only vendors with a physical presence in a state can be required to collect use tax. Thus tax evasion is common on interstate sales to households.

The decision in *Quill* produces a result that is indefensible from an economic point of view: local merchants that charge sales tax must compete with remote vendors that need not collect use tax, and state and local governments lose tax revenue from remote sales.[21] The Supreme Court required the physical presence test because it thought that state (and local) taxes were so dissimilar that requiring vendors lacking a physical presence in the market state to collect use tax would impose an unconstitutional burden on interstate commerce. Although the *Quill* decision applies explicitly to sales of tangible products, it is unclear whether it would also apply to sales of digital content.

By exercising its power to regulate interstate commerce, Con-

20. See Walter Hellerstein, "State Taxation of Electronic Commerce," *Tax Law Review* 52 (spring 1997): 425–505.
21. See also McLure, "Taxation of Electronic Commerce."

gress could override the Court's decision in *Quill*. It is unclear whether the states can get around *Quill* at this late date by simplifying their systems of sales and use taxes; given the Court's emphasis on *stare decisis* ("let the decision stand") and the need for "settled expectations," congressional ratification of state action might be required.

It is worth noting the following sources of complexity of state and local sales and use taxes:

- Some 7,600 local jurisdictions in the United States levy sales and use taxes; not all local jurisdictions in a given state levy tax at the same rate. Thus, if required to collect local use tax, remote vendors would need to know both the locality of destination of a sale and the tax rate applied there.

- Boundaries of taxing jurisdictions do not neatly correspond to those of postal ZIP codes.

- States (and localities in a few states) are free to define the sales and use tax base as they wish; they need not tax the same products, employ the same definitions of products, or provide the same exemptions for products sold to businesses or nonprofit organizations.

- Administrative procedures (registration, filing, payment of tax, appeals, etc.) vary from state to state.

- There is no central multistate administrative organization to which remote vendors can report; vendors must report separately to each state in which they have a duty to collect use tax (and to individual local governments in some states).

- States that attempt to force remote vendors to collect use tax have not enacted realistic *de minimis* rules that would exempt remote vendors making only small amounts of sales in the state from the duty to collect.

- Vendors discounts (the privilege of retaining a small part of revenues collected, which states allow as partial compensation for the costs of collecting sales tax) fall woefully short of costs of compliance for small firms—and would be especially inadequate for remote vendors, who would encounter particularly high costs of compliance.

Except for *Quill,* the resulting complexity would be onerous for both firms engaged in traditional remote selling (e.g., mail order) and firms engaged in electronic commerce. The burden of compliance would be much worse for small firms engaged in electronic commerce since—leaving aside the potential barrier created by the difficulty of compliance with use taxes—small firms can engage in electronic commerce much more effectively than in conventional direct marketing. Whereas large firms might be able to deal with the complexity and the high compliance costs associated with the hodgepodge of state and local use taxes, small firms might find interstate sales uneconomical if the duty to collect use tax were expanded, without substantial simplification.

THE PECULIAR CASE OF TELECOMMUNICATIONS AND INTERNET ACCESS

For historical reasons telecommunications are taxed far more heavily than most other goods and services.[22] Local excises have been justified as compensation for the use of the public right-of-way and for the monopoly position once enjoyed by the phone company. By comparison, as a service, Internet access ordinarily has not been subject to sales taxes during its short existence (but providers of Internet access may pay tax on their purchases of

---

22. Walter Hellerstein, "Telecommunications and Electronic Commerce: Overview and Appraisal," *State Tax Notes* 12, no. 7 (February 17, 1997): 519–26.

equipment and telecommunications, which ordinarily do not qualify for resale exemptions). This situation is anomalous because providers of telecommunications and Internet access increasingly compete with each other. Moreover, following the dramatic technical innovations that make competition and the deregulation of telecommunications possible, it is difficult to find a sound reason for taxing that service more heavily than other goods and services.

THE SCOPE OF DISCUSSION

Participants in the debate on the application of sales and use taxes to electronic commerce do not agree on the proper scope of the debate.[23] Some would limit the discussion to electronic commerce in digital content and Internet access, taking the present tax treatment of sales by local merchants and of remote sales of tangible products as given. Others argue that it is unrealistic to limit the debate in this way, since (a) digital content downloaded from the Internet substitutes for tangible products in many applications, (b) electronic commerce in tangible products and other remote sales are often in direct competition, and (c) Internet access and telecommunications are becoming increasingly intertwined and indistinguishable. Many would expand the discussion to include taxation of all remote vendors and/or telecommunications but not the taxation of traditional commerce. Still others believe that this is a once-in-a-lifetime opportunity to rationalize the state sales and use tax by exempting all sales to business, expanding the tax base to include most services and intangible products sold to households, which are now largely exempt, and eliminating special taxes on telecommunications.

It seems that not all questions of scope need to be answered the same way. For example, it is hard to see how the tax base of a given state can sensibly be defined differently for remote and local commerce. But it might be feasible, absent constitutional restrictions,

23. McLure, "Achieving a Level Playing Field."

to impose different tax rates on a given product being sold locally and in remote commerce. (It seems unlikely that, failing congressional sanction, the Supreme Court would allow a statewide use tax to be applied to remote sales to a locality that had no sales tax on the same product.)

PROPOSALS FOR SALES AND USE TAXATION
OF ELECTRONIC COMMERCE

Most proposals for the application of sales and use taxes to electronic commerce take as given the objective of imposing destination-based taxation. But a few, noting the extreme difficulty of achieving this objective, favor origin-based taxation.

Proposals for Destination-Based Taxation. Destination-based taxation requires that remote vendors collect use tax. But for this to be a reasonable demand, as well as a realistic possibility politically, state sales and use taxes must be greatly simplified. Among the simplifications advocated by various participants in the National Tax Association (NTA) Project (described below) are the following:[24] (a) one tax rate per state; (b) attribution of sales only to the state level; (c) uniform rules for determining the situs of sales (the ship-to address for tangible products and the billing address for digital content); (d) a uniform "menu" of what might be taxed, from which each state could choose its tax base; (e) adequate notice of changes in tax base and tax rates; (f) uniform administrative procedures; (g) a simplified system of filing; and (h) a *de minimis* rule. Some of these involve political or technical problems that deserve discussion.

One Rate per State/Attribution to State Level. The requirement of one rate per state, combined with attribution of sales only to the state level, which business says is vital, would seriously un-

---

24. National Tax Association Communications and Electronic Commerce Tax Project, "Final Report."

dermine the fiscal autonomy of local governments. Local government officials would not be satisfied to rely on state governments
to channel revenues from the uniform local portion of a sales and
use tax to local governments. Moreover, this solution would immediately raise practical problems for local governments that have
pledged revenues from sales and use taxes to finance debt service
for capital projects (e.g., stadiums). The hypothetical solution of
divorcing the use tax rate from the sales tax rate might be an acceptable compromise, if not a pretty one. But, besides being questionable politically, it risks constitutional challenge, unless endorsed by Congress.

Menu of Potentially Taxable/Exempt Sales.   Because members
of the NTA Project were unwilling to propose unification of the
state sales tax base, they suggested the menu approach. A uniform
menu of potentially taxable products would represent a substantial
simplification, but it would not be simple or easy to implement,
especially in the case of catalog sales. (Those who wish to pay by
check, predominantly the poor and the elderly, pose the greatest
problem, as they need to be able to calculate the tax due when they
place an order. In the case of payments made by credit card, the
vendor can calculate the tax or adjust calculations made by the
buyer.) Preliminary investigation suggests that there might be up-
wards of ten thousand items in such a menu.[25] Besides "off/on"
switches to indicate whether a given product is taxable or exempt
when sold to households, it might be appropriate to have similar
menus and switches to indicate the tax treatment of sales to busi-

25. See United Nations, "Central Product Classification (CPC)," Version 1.0,
Statistical Papers, Series M, No. 77, Ver. 1.0, 1998, available at www.un.org/
Depts/unsd/class/cpcad.

ness and tax-exempt organizations; the NTA Project did not consider this question.[26]

Simplified Filing. The NTA Project examined two forms of simplified filing, plus a "hybrid" that draws on the others to modify present practice. None seems to be a panacea.

Under the *base-state approach*, adapted from the International Fuel Tax Agreement, a vendor lacking a physical presence in a state would file a use tax return (and pay tax due) for that state with its "base state" (presumably where it has its primary place of business), instead of with individual states where it makes remote sales. A central clearinghouse would calculate net interstate liabilities.

The base-state system has several obvious faults. First, tax administrators in each base state would need to be familiar with the tax laws of all states in which their taxpayers make remote sales— a daunting task, even with use of a uniform menu to define tax bases.[27] (By comparison, the definition of the base of motor fuel taxes is relatively simple.) Moreover, tax administrators in base states would have little incentive to collect revenues that would go to other states.

A *real-time system* would rely on financial institutions to collect use tax at the time a sale is made, based on the nature of the product, the applicable tax rate in the state of destination, and the nature of the buyer (household, business, or tax-exempt organization). The requirement that the computers of these institutions contain the tax bases and rates of each state and each local jurisdiction, and even the tax treatment of business purchasers and tax-exempt organizations, does not seem overwhelming. Under present prac-

---

26. I propose to exempt essentially all sales to business. My proposal does not cover sales to nonprofit organizations.

27. My proposal to the ACEC would overcome this problem by requiring that all states adopt the same tax base.

tice, however, vendors submit substantially less information to financial institutions than would be required to implement the real-time system—essentially the account numbers of the merchant and the buyer and the total amount of the sale, including applicable tax. To modify these systems to accommodate the real-time system would require a major investment, for which financial institutions would reasonably expect to receive compensation. (Because of savings in costs of compliance and administration, this might be a bargain in the long run.) Moreover, concerns about privacy—and legislation already on the books in some states—could impede use of this system and even the identification of the state of billing address required by the hybrid system.

The *hybrid system* would depart less from present practice. Certain functions (e.g., registration) might be consolidated, as in the base-state system, but filing would continue to be done on a state-by-state basis. States might rely on financial institutions to provide or verify the state in the purchaser's billing address but not to collect tax.

On behalf of the National Governors' Association (NGA), Governor Michael Leavitt of Utah has proposed that the ACEC consider a voluntary system in which "trusted third parties" would calculate, collect, and remit use tax.[28] In the same spirit as the real-time system considered by the NTA, the NGA proposal could build on existing systems.[29]

Proposals for Origin-Based Taxation. Noting the complexity of destination-based taxation and the need for federal legislation

28. See "Streamlined Sales Tax System for the 21st Century," available at www.ecommercecommission.org.

29. See, for example, TAXWARE International, Inc., "Adapting Tax Technology to the Internet—the eCommerce Transaction Tax Server," submission to the Advisory Commission on Electronic Commerce, available at www.ecommercecommission.org.

to implement it, some have argued that taxation of electronic commerce in digitized content—or perhaps of all remote commerce—should be based on the origin principle.[30] Although clearly feasible, this approach encounters the objections voiced earlier (inconsistency with the basic destination-based system, a race to the bottom, and distortion of locational decisions).

THE REVENUE AT STAKE

Some advocates of extending the sales and use tax to electronic commerce have called the state sales tax "road-kill on the information superhighway."[31] But as long as intrastate sales do not become tax exempt, the assertion that "the sky is not falling" seems more accurate, at least for now.[32] The lost-revenue scenario is rosy for the following reasons. First, an estimated 80 percent of sales in electronic commerce are from one business to another; many of these transactions are explicitly exempt, and use tax is currently being collected on many of the rest. Second, a substantial share of electronic commerce sales to households involves services (e.g., travel and financial services), intangibles, or goods (e.g., groceries and prescription drugs) that are not subject to sales and use taxes. Finally, some electronic commerce involves sales to households di-

30. See Andrew Wagner and Wade Anderson, "Origin-Based Taxation of Electronic Commerce," *State Tax Notes* 17, no. 3 (July 19, 1999): 187–92; Terry Ryan and Eric Miethke, "The Seller-State Option: Solving the Electronic Commerce Dilemma," *State Tax Notes* (October 5, 1998): 881–92, and references provided there.

31. Nathan Newman, "Prop 13 Meets the Internet: How State and Local Government Finances Are Becoming Road Kill on the Information Superhighway," Economic Democracy Information Network Report, University of California, Berkeley, Center for Community Economic Research, August 1995.

32. Robert J. Cline and Thomas S. Neubig, "The Sky Is Not Falling: Why State and Local Revenues Were Not Significantly Impacted by the Internet in 1998," Ernst & Young Economics Consulting and Quantitative Analysis, June 18, 1999; see also Goolsbee and Zittrain, "Evaluating the Costs and Benefits of Taxing Internet Commerce."

verted from other remote vendors that lack a duty to collect use tax. In other words, revenue loss would be small primarily because the present system falls far short of the ideal. In brief, the failure to tax electronic commerce would be "no big deal" because a substantial amount of revenue comes from sales to business, which would be taxed, even though they should not be; most services would not be taxed, as they should be, even if provided locally; and most remote sales to households are already effectively exempt, contrary to common sense, as well as the widely accepted model of destination-based taxation. The last two points suggest that the real revenue problem lies not in electronic commerce per se but in the failure to tax services and the effective tax exemption of most remote commerce.

Some who favor preferential taxation of electronic commerce deny that electronic commerce poses any threat to Main Street business, noting the large fraction of businesses that now have a presence on the Internet. But there may be some very large and nasty flies in this seemingly optimistic ointment. First, suppose that households in New York order furniture (or other tangible products) from stores in New Jersey and vice versa, for delivery or drop shipment by common carrier; on big-ticket items, the savings from evading the use tax could be significant. It is possible, if not likely, that there would be no net effect on total business in either of the two states. But both states would be deprived of revenue they would receive if the sales were made by local merchants. The de facto tax exemption provided by *Quill* could finance a great deal of unproductive cross-hauling of merchandise across state lines.

Second, the courts of some states have ruled that a firm engaged in remote selling does not necessarily have nexus for use tax purposes just because an affiliated company has a physical presence in the state. Already many of the nation's largest retailers are establishing separate subsidiaries to handle Internet sales. This could lead to the migration of substantial amounts of commerce from

Main Street merchants, which collect sales tax, to out-of-state affiliates engaged in electronic commerce, which would not collect use tax. In that case, revenue loss from the exemption of electronic commerce might be far greater than commonly assumed.[33]

Any revenue losses discussed thus far pale beside those in the worst-case scenario—exemption of electronic commerce from sales taxes as well as use taxes. Senator John McCain (R.-Ariz.) has introduced legislation that would amend the Internet Freedom Act (ITFA) so that state and local governments could not impose "sales or use taxes for domestic or foreign goods or services acquired through electronic commerce." Congressmen John Kasich and John Boehner (both R.-Ohio) have proposed a virtually identical prohibition.

The proposed legislation relies implicitly on the definition of electronic commerce contained in the ITFA:

> Electronic commerce.—The term "electronic commerce" means any transaction conducted over the Internet or through Internet access, comprising the sale, lease, license, offer, or delivery of property, goods, services, or information, whether or not for consideration, and includes the provision of Internet access.

The exemption proposed by McCain, Kasich, and Boehner would effectively eliminate the sales tax. To gain the exemption for a purchase made at a store on Main Street, all a customer would need to do is route the transaction from a terminal in the store to the Internet and back. Andrew Pincus, the representative of the U.S. Commerce Department on the ACEC, identified this problem during the commission's meetings in San Francisco on December 14, 1999:

33. For a detailed discussion of the lack of "nexus by affiliation," see Michael J. McIntyre, "Taxing Electronic Commerce Fairly and Efficiently," *Tax Law Review* 52 (1997): 625–54.

As long as they order it over the kiosk, they just go to the checkout counter and it's delivered to them and they pay for it and they've used the Internet. . . . In a year or two, wouldn't every store owner of any size in America have integrated the Internet into their business in a way that there wouldn't be any sales tax?

Under this scenario, the sales tax would become roadkill.

THE NATIONAL TAX ASSOCIATION PROJECT

Beginning in the fall of 1997, the National Tax Association (NTA) convened its Communications and Electronic Commerce Tax Project (the NTA Project) "to develop a broadly available public report which identifies and explores the issues involved in applying state and local taxes and fees to electronic commerce and which makes recommendations to state and local officials regarding the application of such taxes."[34] Focusing first on the sales and use tax, the project's Steering Committee, composed of sixteen representatives from business and sixteen from government, as well as seven others (including the author), quickly specified the broad outlines of a possible compromise—an expanded duty to collect use tax, in exchange for substantial simplification. The Steering Committee identified and discussed many elements of simplification, including those described earlier, and in September 1999 it approved a final report that analyzes issues and describes areas of tentative agreement and disagreement.[35] It was unable, however, to agree on a legislative proposal because it had previously agreed that "nothing is agreed to until everything is agreed to." (It might be noted that a three-fourths majority of the Steering Committee is required to approve any measure.) This report should serve a useful

34. "Description of the Organization and Operation of the Communications and Electronic Commerce Tax Project," available at www.ntanet.org.
35. National Tax Association Communications and Electronic Commerce Tax Project, "Final Report."

educational purpose and provide valuable input to the Advisory Commission on Electronic Commerce.[36]

THE ADVISORY COMMISSION ON ELECTRONIC COMMERCE

In October 1998 the U.S. Congress enacted the Internet Tax Freedom Act (ITFA). Besides imposing a three-year moratorium on new taxes on the Internet, the ITFA created the Advisory Commission on Electronic Commerce, which is composed of eight representatives from business, eight from state and local governments, and three from the federal government. A two-thirds majority is required for decisions of the Commission. The charge of the ACEC included whether to impose sales and use taxes on electronic commerce.

Prospects that the ACEC will be able to produce a consensus report on sales and use taxation do not appear bright. First, the NTA Project demonstrates just how difficult agreement will be. Second, almost none of the Commission's members are tax experts; rapid mastery of a complex subject is thus required. Third, although some members of the Commission believe that electronic commerce should be taxed, a substantial fraction of the membership would prefer continuation—and perhaps codification—of the status quo, which leaves remote commerce tax free, unless the vendor has nexus in the taxing state.[37]

The Commission did not hold its first meeting until June 1999, almost halfway through its eighteen-month statutory life. Despite the critical shortage of time, much of the meeting, held in Williamsburg, Virginia, was consumed in bureaucratic wrangling and polit-

36. For a more detailed discussion of the deliberations of the NTA Project, see McLure, "Electronic Commerce and the State Retail Sales Tax," pp. 208–15.

37. In McLure, "Electronic Commerce and the State Retail Sales Tax," p. 208, the author suggests that "asking this Commission whether Internet access and electronic commerce should be subject to the same taxes imposed on local business is analogous [*sic*] entrusting a commission of foxes to guard the henhouse."

ical posturing, rather than being devoted to serious discussion of substantive issues. Reflecting the predilections of the chairman of the Commission, Governor James Gilmore of Virginia, many of the presentations were little more than lobbying for exemption of electronic commerce based on ideological presuppositions, rather than unbiased discussions of whether and how electronic commerce should be taxed. Only at its second meeting, in New York City in September 1999, which was cut short by the impending arrival of a hurricane and the need for Governor Gilmore to return to Virginia, did the Commission agree to ask for proposals that would entail "radical simplification" of the sales and use tax—long recognized to be the sine qua non of any solution involving an expanded duty to collect use tax. Again there was little serious discussion of alternatives. At its third meeting, in San Francisco in December 1999, the Commission finally heard proposals for radical simplification, along with more arguments for exempting electronic commerce. Only one more meeting is scheduled, in March 2000, a month before the Commission is scheduled to expire.

Given the complexity of the issues the Commission faces and the dearth of empirical evidence on which to base policy decisions, at least one group has suggested that the life of the Commission should be extended to the end of 2000.[38] The Commission did not discuss this issue in San Francisco.

THE VIEW FROM SILICON VALLEY

It would be wrong to believe that everyone involved in electronic commerce thinks that e-commerce should be tax exempt. I cite two compelling pieces of evidence. The first is the view of the participants in the Hoover symposium reported in this volume. As

38. "Establishing a Framework to Evaluate E-Commerce Tax Policy Options," a report on an e-commerce taxation workshop held at the University of California at Berkeley on October 1, 1999, released December 14, 1999.

the Introduction states, "A substantial consensus prevailed that all distribution channels—mail, telephone, Internet, as well as remote and local sellers—should be subject to consistent sales and use taxes." This echos the view stated more fully in the November 1998 report of the Electronic Commerce Advisory Council (ECAC) appointed by Republican governor Pete Wilson.[39] Like the participants in the Hoover symposium, the members of the California ECAC were predominantly from firms involved in various aspects of electronic commerce.

Both groups expressed considerable reservations about the feasibility of imposing a duty to collect use tax on those involved in electronic commerce in digital content and services. While some might find this self-serving, it is undoubtedly true that the anonymity of the Internet makes compliance and administration much more difficult than for electronic commerce in tangible goods.

SOME CAVEATS: DUBIOUS ARGUMENTS

Before leaving the discussion of the state sales and use tax it is appropriate to warn the reader of arguments that the author believes to be fallacious. Most involve failure to apply elementary economics correctly.

"Remote vendors do not consume services." Some argue that remote vendors should not be required to collect use taxes because they do not consume public services provided by the market state. This view reflects a misunderstanding of the benefit principle of taxation. The sales and use tax is levied primarily to finance services provided to households, not to finance services provided to business firms doing business in the taxing state. Thus it should apply equally to all taxable goods and services consumed in the

---

39. This report, entitled "If I'm So Empowered, Why Do I Need You? Defining Government's Role in Internet Electronic Commerce," is available at www.e-commerce.ca.gov/1a_cover.html.

state, not only to those sold by local merchants. (The invalidity of the argument cited above can be seen by replacing reference to the sales and use tax with reference to an excise on tobacco products used to finance health care for smokers. No one would seriously suggest that cigarettes sent by mail order from another state should not be taxed just because they are sold by a vendor that receives few services in the taxing state.)[40]

"Shipping and handling compensate for the lack of use tax." Some argue that the need to pay charges for shipping and handling, which are higher for shipments to individual customers than for bulk shipments to local merchants, compensates for the lack of use tax on remote sales. This argument is obviously invalid in the case of digitized content; there are no shipping and handling charges to offset the lack of use tax. But it is equally invalid in the case of tangible products. The easy case involves a comparison of two remote vendors, one with nexus and one without. Shipping and handling costs may be comparable, but one collects tax and the other does not. Finally, consider the more difficult case, a remote vendor compared with a Main Street merchant. If costs are higher for remote commerce, that is prima facie evidence that the tax exemption induces economic inefficiency; costs are being incurred that would not exist if tax policy were neutral.

The previous two arguments (involving lack of services to remote vendors and shipping costs) may not be convincing to non-economists. But consider the following. Suppose someone suggested that sales (or use) tax should be collected when Americans buy foreign-made cars from American merchants but not when

40. An admittedly unrealistic example illustrates the argument. Suppose that it were possible to sell motor fuel in a state without having a physical presence there. Suppose further that a tax on motor fuels consumed by motorists in the state is used to finance the construction and maintenance of roads and highways in the state. Should fuel sold in the state by a remote vendor be taxed? Of course it should; the tax is intended to charge for the in-state motorist's use of highways.

they order them directly from a foreign manufacturer—or that sales tax should be collected on cars made in the United States but not on cars made abroad. Few would think these suggestions make sense. Yet they are exactly analogous to arguments that purchases from out-of-state vendors should not be taxed; that is, foreign merchants and car manufacturers do not consume services provided by the American states and they incur substantial shipping costs getting their products to American markets. Yet we do not consider either fact in deciding whether to collect sales or use tax on foreign-made cars.

"Taxing electronic commerce would hinder the growth of small e-commerce firms." No sensible proposal to impose an expanded duty to collect use tax would negatively affect small e-commerce vendors. First, there would be a *de minimis* exemption that would eliminate the duty to collect for small vendors. Second, the author's proposal to eliminate tax on sales to business implies that taxes on such vendors would be lower, not higher.

"Main Street merchants are going on-line." There are at least three reasons not to draw solace from the fact that many Main Street merchants are joining the stampede to electronic commerce. First, this is small comfort to local merchants that do not establish an on-line presence, likely to be the smallest and most vulnerable. Second, unless local merchants that go on-line place the electronic commerce aspects of business in a separate subsidiary incorporated in another state, they must charge sales tax. The need to isolate on-line business in a separate out-of-state corporation distorts business operations because, for one thing, accepting refunds at the Main Street location is likely to create nexus for the e-commerce affiliate. Third, if the on-line strategy is successful, revenue losses will be far greater than the optimistic scenarios that assume that not much taxable consumption spending shifts to the Internet.

"The European Union is shifting to origin-based taxation." Some suggest that it would be appropriate to apply origin-based

taxation to electronic commerce because the European Union (EU) is shifting from destination-based taxation to origin-based taxation under the value-added tax (VAT). Nothing could be further from the truth.[41] The EU has recently determined that digital content downloaded from the Internet should be taxed as a supply of services. For historical reasons services have been subject to origin-based taxation in the EU. (They have not been exempt, as in the typical American states sales tax.) But the EU has recently decided to move to destination-based taxation of services, in large part to prevent the loss of revenue implied by origin-based taxation. Thus, like goods and other services, digital content will be subject to destination-based taxation.

"It is not necessary to tax electronic commerce because the states have surpluses." This assertion reflects an implicit assumption that taxation of electronic commerce would be the source of additional revenue—that taxing electronic commerce would increase taxes. (This assumption is encouraged by the lament of state and local officials that revenues will drop if electronic commerce is not taxed.) I believe that this is not the way to frame the issue— that it makes much more sense to discuss the taxation of electronic commerce in a revenue-neutral context. In that context, the existence of a surplus is irrelevant; rates could be lower if e-commerce is taxed than if it is not.

"The development of electronic commerce is driving the recent economic expansion." Some attribute the recent expansion of the American economy to the development of electronic commerce and infer from that that electronic commerce should be exempt.[42] First, no evidence is offered to support the proposition, other than the

41. The statement of Michel Aujean, director of Tax Policy at the European Commission, before the ACEC on December 14, 1999, should dispel any remaining doubts on this score.

42. See, for example, the comments by Governor Gilmore at the San Francisco meeting of the ACEC.

fact that the two phenomena are occurring simultaneously. This fallacy would not pass muster in any undergraduate economics course in the country, let alone a graduate course in econometrics. One might just as well—and with as much basis in hard evidence—attribute the expansion to the decline in the murder rate in New York City, the decline in the teenage pregnancy rate, or the decline in the fortunes of the Notre Dame football team, all of which are also contemporaneous with it. Electronic commerce may indeed be one factor that is fueling the expansion. But parsing out its contribution requires a careful econometric analysis that attempts to control systematically for other influences that are occurring simultaneously, a difficult enterprise that would challenge the best econometricians; it is not something that can be achieved by casual observation.

Second, and more important, even if it is true that the rise of electronic commerce is fueling the expansion, the logical conclusion is not that all electronic commerce should be exempt but that all sales to business should be exempt. Consider figure 1, which shows a four-way division of commerce among (a) electronic and traditional commerce and (b) sales to business and sales to households. Cell 1, business-to-business transactions in electronic commerce—sometimes called B2B—is where most electronic commerce is occurring. It is also the source of most of the gains in productivity attributable to electronic commerce. By comparison,

	Electronic commerce	Traditional commerce
Sales to business	1. Electronic sales to business	2. Traditional sales to business
Sales to households	3. Electronic sales to households	4. Traditional sales to households

Figure 1. Four-Way Division of Commerce

electronic sales to households (cell 3) are relatively small and not likely to be the source of great gains in productivity.

This figure assists in understanding the difference between my proposal and the proposal to exempt all electronic commerce. I would exempt all sales to business—the first row of the figure— whereas an exemption for all electronic commerce would apply to the first column. Both proposals exempt the crucial B2B segment of electronic commerce. My proposal would also exempt nonelectronic B2B transactions, as is appropriate for a conceptually sensible and simple sales tax; it would not exempt electronic commerce with households. An exemption for all electronic commerce would discriminate against traditional commerce, distorting economic choices and creating inequities.[43]

Norms, Practices, and Proposals: National Income Taxation

In the United States most attention has focused on application of the state sales and use tax to electronic commerce. But there is also a lively discussion of whether and how the income taxes levied by national governments can adapt to electronic commerce, largely in a forum provided by the OECD.[44]

NORMS FOR TAXATION OF INTERNATIONAL FLOWS OF INCOME

Economists generally posit two standards for the taxation of international flows of income.[45]

43. Discussions of "dubious arguments" are adapted from McLure, "How— and Why—the States Should Tax Electronic Commerce," *State Tax Notes* (January 10, 2000): 129.

44. There are also debates involving two other taxes: the value-added tax imposed in the European Union and elsewhere and the income taxes imposed by the American states; see generally McLure, "Taxation of Electronic Commerce." On international income taxation and the VAT, see the web site of the Fiscal and Financial Committee of the OECD at www.oecd.org/daf/. Debates on subnational taxation similar to those in the United States are also occurring in Canada.

45. See McLure, "Taxation of Electronic Commerce," pp. 351–62, and refer-

Under *capital export neutrality* the tax paid does not depend on whether capital is employed at home or abroad. It is achieved (a) if taxation is based only on the residence of the taxpayer or (b) if income is taxed by both the source and the residence countries, but residence countries allow foreign tax credits (FTCs) for taxes paid to source countries. Residence-based taxation has the advantage that it does not distort the choice of where to invest. Moreover, it is consistent with efforts by residence countries to tax uniformly the worldwide income of their taxpayers.

Under *capital import neutrality* the tax paid does not depend on whether capital invested in a given country comes from domestic investors or abroad. It is achieved if taxation is levied only by the source country (that is, where investment occurs). Unlike residence-based taxation, source-based taxation can distort the choice of where to invest and is not consistent with taxation of worldwide income by countries of residence.

OVERVIEW OF PRACTICE:
TAXATION OF INTERNATIONAL FLOWS OF INCOME

Taxation based only on the source of income or the residence of taxpayers is rare. Virtually all nations impose income tax on income deemed to have its source within their jurisdiction. In addition, many nations, including the United States, also tax the worldwide income of their residents, providing FTCs for income taxes paid to source countries. But it is common to respect the legal distinctions between parent and foreign subsidiaries. Thus a parent corporation operating in a country that taxes worldwide income ordinarily pays tax on foreign-source income earned by a subsidi-

ences provided there; Richard Doernberg and Luc Hinnekens, *Electronic Commerce and International Taxation* (The Hague: Kluwer Law International, 1999); David E. Hardesty, *Electronic Commerce: Taxation and Planning* (Boston: Warren, Gorham, and Lamont, 1999); and Frances M. Horner and Jeffrey Owens, "Tax and the Web: New Technology, Old Problems," *Bulletin for International Fiscal Documentation* 50 (1996): 516–23.

ary only when such income is distributed as dividends. (Countries that rely solely on source-based taxation may not tax dividends.) The deferral of tax implied in this treatment means that capital export neutrality is not fully achieved—that there is an important element of source-based taxation that is not offset by current residence-based taxation.

Deferral also means that tax havens are possible. Transactions are structured in such a way as to attribute income to a tax haven country, where it is subject to little or no taxation. Many developed countries have legislation intended to deter the use of tax havens to minimize tax; such legislation commonly specifies that, under certain conditions, the tax on the income of controlled foreign corporations (CFCs) will not be deferred.

The Nature and Source of Income.   To apply source-based taxation (and to calculate limits on foreign tax credits, which ordinarily are limited to the amount of tax that would be due in the home country), it is necessary to know the geographic source of income. Under existing international tax rules, which are based largely on the OECD Model Treaty, the nature of income determines the deemed source of income.

Net income from the sale of goods is taxed where it originates, provided it is related to a *permanent establishment* (PE) maintained by the taxpayer in the country. A fixed place of business or the use of a dependent agent may indicate the existence of a PE. A facility maintained solely for the storage, display, or delivery of goods or merchandise is not a PE.

Income from the supply of services is taxed where services are performed, provided the taxpayer has a PE in the taxing country or is physically present there. Payments for the use of intangible property (for example, royalties) commonly are not subject to income tax in the source country but may be subject to withholding taxes.

Separate Accounting and the Arm's Length Standard.   To divide the income of a multinational corporation (MNC) among the constituent parts (affiliated firms) making up the MNC, nations employ separate accounting and the arm's length standard. That is, each separately incorporated member of a group of affiliated corporations is treated as a separate entity for tax purposes, and the transfer prices used to value transactions between affiliates are those that would prevail in transactions between unrelated parties. Traditionally the arm's length test of transfer prices has been based on comparable uncontrolled prices, cost plus (a margin), or resale price (minus a margin). The growing importance of intangible assets has made the use of these methods increasingly untenable because there commonly is no external market for intangibles. Thus increased reliance has been placed on "profit splits" (division of profits among the affiliates contributing to the creation of the profits). Unlike what the OECD calls the "predetermined formulas" employed to divide the income of American multistate firms among the states in which they operate, formulas used in calculating profit splits are intended both to reflect the situation of individual taxpayers and to tease out the profit arising from individual transactions.

IMPLICATIONS OF ELECTRONIC COMMERCE
FOR INCOME TAXATION

Electronic commerce blurs the distinctions inherent in the above descriptions, complicates transfer pricing, and hinders tax administration.

Nature of Income. Traditional distinctions between types of income are blurred in a world of electronic commerce. For example, provision of a database might be considered to be the sale of a good (if a book is provided), supply of a service (if the supplier must manipulate the data to conform to the needs of the customer), or provision of an intangible (if the customer downloads the data).[46] Distinctions that may have made sense in a world of tangible products are inadequate for a world of intangible products.

It can be argued that such indistinct distinctions should not determine the tax treatment of transactions—that distinctions should be more robust or should be eliminated as meaningless. Since eliminating distinctions between types of income would undermine the present system, most efforts have been devoted to making the distinctions more robust. It has been suggested, for example, that performance of nonministerial functions by humans is required for the provision of a service—that machines that merely perform ministerial functions are not performing services.[47] The U.S. Treasury Department, in software regulations, has suggested concentrating on the rights transferred in determining the nature of income.

Permanent Establishment.   There has been considerable discussion of what constitutes a permanent establishment in a world of electronic commerce. For example, should the presence of a server—or even a web page—that displays goods and services and receives orders be viewed as a PE—especially since the server could just as easily be located in another country without loss of function? Should a test of economic presence replace the physical presence test of the PE? In a proposed clarification of Article 5 of its Model Treaty, the OECD has suggested that the web page of a vendor would not constitute a PE but that a server owned and operated by the taxpayer would constitute a PE if it has a fixed

46. Similar ambiguities exist in the case of software, but in the United States these have recently been addressed in regulations that may suggest the way traditional distinctions will be implemented in other lines of electronic commerce in digital content.

47. See Peter Glichlich, Howard J. Levine, Sanford H. Goldberg, and Ellen S. Brody, "Electronic Services: Suggesting a Man-Machine Distinction," *Journal of Taxation* 87 (1997): 69–75.

location in the taxing country and is used in the business of the taxpayer.[48]

Transfer Pricing. The spread of electronic commerce *within* MNCs also complicates matters. Contrast the situation in which tangible products (for example, components of computers) are transferred a few times from one affiliate to another in the process of production and assembly with the situation in which software in the process of being developed and written is transferred around the globe two or three times a day, to be written where the sun is shining. Several differences are obvious. First, whereas the individual computer components may have a market value, the individual contributions to the computer program probably do not. Second, whereas transactions in the tangible product are relatively few and identifiable, those involving the computer program are many and hard to identify. Third, application of transactional analysis to determine a profit split may be virtually impossible in the case of the computer program.

Administration. As noted earlier, tax administration will be difficult in a world where buyers and sellers cannot be identified, digital products can be sold without a physical presence in the country, the taxpayer is located in a tax haven, and payment can be made using money that cannot be traced.

INCREASED RELIANCE ON RESIDENCE-BASED TAXATION

Problems such as those just described have led the U.S. Treasury to suggest that it may be necessary and appropriate to shift primary reliance from source-based taxation of business income to residence-based taxation. Critics have found this proposal naive, as well as self-serving. They note that residence-based taxation is not without problems; at the very least legislation dealing with

---

48. The proposed modifications to Article 5 are available at www.oecd.org/daf/fa/first_en.

controlled foreign corporations would probably need to be tightened.[49] Beyond that, there would be a shift of revenue to the United States, by far the leading residence of firms engaged in electronic commerce. It does not seem that this suggestion will soon be accepted. But the ability to conduct sales over the Internet without the existence of a PE in the market country is likely to reduce revenues of source countries in any event.

INCREASED RELIANCE ON FORMULAS TO APPORTION INCOME

Another alternative is to shift from reliance on separate accounting and the arm's length standard to greater reliance on formula apportionment to divide the income of multinational corporations among the nations in which they operate. Under formula apportionment, distinctions between income from the sale of goods, income from the supply of services, and income from the provision of intangibles are irrelevant, and transfer pricing problems vanish. But a shift to formula apportionment would be ironic, as well as drastic, considering how hard foreign governments and taxpayers fought against state use of worldwide unitary taxation during the early 1980s. (Unitary taxation is the name commonly given to the practice under which some states "combine" the activities of affiliates deemed to be engaged in a unitary business for the purpose of applying their apportionment formulas. Worldwide combination extended the practice to all affiliates, no matter where located.) As recently as 1992, a committee of experts appointed by the Commission of the European Communities rejected formula apportionment as a substitute for separate accounting.[50]

49. See Reuven Avi-Yonah, "International Taxation of Electronic Commerce," *Tax Law Review* 52 (spring 1997): 507–55.

50. Commission of the European Communities, *Report of the Committee of Independent Experts on Company Taxation* (Luxembourg: Commission of the European Communities, March 1992).

Proposal

At the request of Governor Michael Leavitt of Utah, the author submitted the following proposal, entitled "Radical Simplification of State Sales and Use Taxes: The Prerequisite for an Expanded Duty to Collect Use Tax on Remote Sales," to the Advisory Commission on Electronic Commerce and presented it at the Commission's meeting in San Francisco on December 15, 1999. It contains an abbreviated statement of the author's views on the proper way to reform state sales and use taxes and thereby resolve the issues reviewed in this chapter.[51]

Preface

The existing state sales and use taxes are a product of their time—a time when *local merchants* sold primarily *tangible products* almost exclusively to *local customers*. They are not suited to the twenty-first century, when *services and intangible products* will be much more important than tangible products and *remote sales* of tangible products and *digitized content*, especially via *electronic commerce*, will be increasingly important. The most obvious problem is complexity:

- Each of forty-six states (including the District of Columbia) chooses its own tax base, with no requirement that the

51. For more complete statements, see Charles E. McLure Jr., "Electronic Commerce and the State Retail Sales Tax: A Challenge to American Federalism"; Charles E. McLure Jr., "How—and Why—the States Should Tax Electronic Commerce"; Charles E. McLure Jr., "Rethinking State and Local Reliance on the Retail Sales Tax: Should We Fix the State Sales Tax or Discard It?" prepared for presentation at a symposium on Electronic Commerce Taxation organized by the Brigham Young University Law Review, January 14, 2000, to be published in the *Brigham Young University Law Review*, forthcoming. A few stylistic changes have been made, and footnotes 53 to 56 have been added; they do not appear in the proposal to the ACEC.

base—or even what might be in the base—be uniform across the nation.

- Each state decides what should be exempt when bought by business.

- Each state sets its own administrative requirements and procedures, including registration, filing of tax returns, payment, audit, and appeals.

- Roughly seven thousand local jurisdictions also levy sales and use taxes.
  —Most local jurisdictions levying sales taxes choose their own tax rates.
  —Local jurisdictions in some states do not follow the state definition of the tax base.
  —Boundaries of local jurisdictions do not correspond to postal ZIP codes.
  —Local governments change their tax rates from time to time, making it difficult for taxpayers[52] to know the current rate.

Because of this complexity, the U.S. Supreme Court, in 1967 (*National Bellas Hess*), and again in 1992 (*Quill*), ruled that a remote vendor could not be required to collect use tax on sales to customers in a state where it lacks a physical presence (nexus). The result is loss of state and local tax revenue, unfair competition for Main Street merchants, and discrimination against those who patronize those merchants, instead of remote vendors—problems that the growth of electronic commerce will aggravate. Sound public policy demands that remote vendors, including those engaged in elec-

---

52. The term *taxpayer* is used (somewhat inaccurately) for both vendors who are legally liable for sales taxes and vendors who (actually or potentially) collect use taxes that legally are due from their customers.

tronic commerce, collect use tax on their sales if those sales exceed a *de minimis* amount. (As Ronald Reagan said in 1981, "The taxing power of government must be used to provide revenues for legitimate government purposes. It must not be used to regulate the economy or bring about social change.") But an expanded duty to collect makes sense only if there is radical simplification of the state sales and use tax "system." This proposal describes a system that would meet this objective and (in the Annex) indicates how the proposed system meets the criteria proposed by the Advisory Commission on Electronic Commerce (ACEC).[53] The proposal is intended to be revenue neutral in each state and locality; tax rates would be raised or lowered, as required to maintain revenues, but not increase revenues.

The Proposal: Summary Statement

This section summarizes the proposals, which are described in detail and justified in the next section.

- There would be a single uniform nationwide base for sales and use tax.
  —The base would consist of all consumption spending by households. Tangible products, services, and intangibles would pay the same tax. Local merchants and remote vendors would collect the same tax.
  —All business purchases would be exempt in all states. There would be a nationally uniform exemption certificate.
- Compliance would be simplified and made less costly for vendors (two options):

53. The annex containing the required certification that the proposal satisfies the criteria announced by the ACEC is omitted.

1. Forms and payments would be filed with one state (base-state approach). A *de minimis* rule would eliminate the duty of some to collect use tax. Realistic vendors' discounts would facilitate "zero-cost" compliance.
2. Trusted third parties (TTPs) would calculate/remit tax (TTP approach). Taxpayers would be subject to joint audits on behalf of all states.

- Software would be used to determine the situs of sales and state and local tax rates.
  —States would certify software and provide it without charge to vendors or TTPs.
  —A "hold-harmless" clause would protect vendors who rely on the software.

In addition to these primary proposals are several "fallback positions" that some may find more politically realistic. The primary proposals provide a benchmark against which to judge other proposals the ACEC may receive, as well as the fallback positions. Because the proposed system is vastly simpler than conceptually defensible alternatives, the need for simplification may drive decision-makers toward it, despite the conventional wisdom that it is politically unrealistic.

The Proposals: Detailed Description and Analysis

THE TAX BASE: GENERAL

Proposal A. All states would define the tax base identically. All sales to households in a state would be subject to tax, whether sold by local merchants or remote vendors, unless there were agreement among all states to exempt certain items (e.g., prescription drugs). Services and intangible products would be subject to tax when bought by households. Special taxes on telecommunications would be eliminated.

The *tax base would be defined uniformly* in all states to simplify compliance and administration. Remote vendors would need to deal with only one definition of the tax base, instead of forty-six (or more, considering local taxes). *All sales to households would be taxed* to prevent erosion of the tax base, simplify the system (e.g., no need to distinguish taxable and exempt food or clothing), avoid distortion of consumer choices, and treat those who buy from local merchants like those who buy from remote vendors. The enormous difficulty in gaining agreement on what should be in the uniform tax base suggests acceptance of the conceptually correct solution: taxing all consumption spending. Worth special note is the avoidance of "indistinct distinctions," such as those between certain tangible products (e.g., shrink-wrapped software, music CDs, and videocassettes) and virtually identical intangible products (software, music, and videos) downloaded from the Internet. Such distinctions complicate compliance and administration and have no economic justification. Including services and intangible products in the tax base would allow reduction of tax rates. There is no justification for special taxes on telecommunications.

Problems with the proposal are primarily political. In addition to the loss of state fiscal sovereignty implied by a uniform tax base, there would be serious opposition to taxation of services and intangible products, even in a revenue-neutral context.

Fallback A1. States might be allowed to choose their own tax bases but be required to define what is or is not subject to tax identically. (Conceptually there would be a menu of commonly defined products, beside which each state would write "taxable" or "exempt.") Computerized "lookup tables" would indicate whether each product is taxed in each state. Bar codes could indicate the product category into which most tangible products fall. To be practical, there should be only a few well-defined product categories—perhaps no more than a dozen. Local jurisdictions should not be allowed to deviate from the state tax base.

The primary proposal involves a radical departure from present practice, in which states choose their own tax bases. The fallback combines greater uniformity than current law with greater state fiscal sovereignty than the primary proposal.

A menu of potentially taxed products might contain about ten thousand products—more or fewer, depending on the degree of aggregation of products. Lookup tables with 460,000 cells (one for each of ten thousand items in forty-six states) are conceptually feasible but perhaps impractical; they would certainly be impractical for catalog sales if the purchaser desires to know the tax due when placing an order. Unless categories were chosen extremely carefully, "indistinct distinctions" and attendant problems would remain.

Fallback A2. It may be politically expedient to provide an exemption for Internet access purchased by households. (Purchases of Internet access by businesses would be exempt under the conceptually correct tax treatment of business purchases, considered below.)

There is little justification for exempting Internet access by households. An exemption would complicate compliance and administration because Internet access is commonly bundled with other (presumably taxable) products, and it would have adverse distributional implications.

THE TAX BASE: EXEMPTION OF BUSINESS PURCHASES

Proposal B. The conceptually correct way to treat business purchases is for all states to treat them identically, by exempting them. (Exemption achieves the same result as under the value-added taxes used in the European Union, where businesses receive a credit for tax paid on purchases.) A uniform exemption certificate should be used throughout the nation.[54]

Uniform treatment of business purchases would simplify compliance and administration; remote sellers would need to know only one set of rules, not forty-six. (The "uniform" exemption certificate drafted by the Multistate Tax Commission is not uniform because state laws are not uniform.) Sellers would not need to judge the eligibility of their customers to make tax-free purchases, depending on the use of the product, as now. *Exemption of business purchases* would eliminate defects of the present system: discrimination among products, distortion of production decisions, incentives for vertical integration, and a tax cost that cannot be recovered on exports. Although exemptions for business purchases (initially available only for resale) have been expanded over time, they remain far from comprehensive. Thus the purchases of some sectors are taxed but those of others are exempt. The proposal would eliminate all such discrimination.

Problems with the proposal are primarily political. In addition to the loss of state fiscal sovereignty, elimination of all business purchases from the tax base would necessitate increasing tax rates to maintain revenue in a revenue-neutral context.[55]

Fallback B. States could continue to decide whether or not to exempt various types of business purchases but be required to define the various types of business purchases that might be exempt identically. (Conceptually there would be a menu of commonly

54. Eligibility for exemption of business purchases could be based on federal income tax law: a purchase would be exempt from sales and use tax if (and only if) it qualifies for a federal income tax deduction (or depreciation allowance, etc.). Since this eligibility is all that need be addressed in a uniform exemption certificate, eligibility could be certified simply by checking a box on a paper order form or clicking on a box in the order form on a web site.

55. If this were the only change, average rates would rise substantially. Taxing services would create an offsetting tendency for rates to fall.

defined types of business purchases, beside which each state would write "taxable" or "exempt.") Computerized lookup tables would indicate tax treatment in each state. To be practical, there should be only a few well-defined categories—perhaps no more than half a dozen. Use of "direct pay" by business customers should be expanded.

This alternative achieves much—but not all—of the simplification of the conceptually ideal proposal, without as much loss of state sovereignty or reduction of tax bases. The adverse economic effects of the present system would remain, but each state would have the option of exempting all categories of business purchases to attract business. Direct pay, which would not be needed under the primary proposal, would reduce the need for vendors to determine whether sales to businesses are for exempt uses.

SOURCING/SITUSING OF SALES AND LOCAL TAX RATES

The situs of remote sales determines the local tax rate to be applied and the jurisdiction that receives tax revenue from a sale. It is thus convenient to consider local tax rates together with the situs of remote sales.

Prefatory Discussion. State sales taxes are based on the destination of sales—or would be, if remote sales were taxed and business inputs were exempt. Unlike origin-based taxation, destination-based taxation avoids distortion of the location of economic activity. Moreover, private consumption is generally a reasonable proxy for the consumption of public services. Thus the conceptually correct way to determine the situs of remote sales is to attribute them to the state and locality of destination of the sale.

Proposal C. Software would be used (a) to determine the state and local tax rates that should be applied to remote sales of particular products and (b) to prepare the reports containing the information needed by states to channel revenues to the appropriate local jurisdictions. Such software would contain rules — to be applied uniformly across the nation—needed to determine the situs of sales not involving tangible products (e.g., for services and telecommunications).

The proposal implements destination-based taxation and provides local governments with autonomy over the tax rate, which would be applied to both sales by local merchants and remote sales. Several qualifications are appropriate. First, states should certify software and enact "hold harmless" rules to protect remote vendors from relatively minor and unintentional errors resulting from good-faith reliance on such software, including those that result from the software vendor's failure to update rate tables. (Local governments should bear the burden of informing providers of software of changes in rates.) Second, such software can be used only for sales to customers that are willing to allow the vendor to calculate the tax and add it to the bill. A special regime may be needed for those who remit by check or money order when placing an order. It might be based on the "one-rate-per-state" fallback position discussed below.

Fallback C. Business representatives argue that remote sales should be attributed ("sourced") only to the state level, claiming that it is impossible to determine accurately the local situs of remote sales. Local governments could set *sales tax* rates, but there would be only one *use tax* rate per state; states would be responsible for allocating revenue from use tax among their local jurisdictions.

The fallback would retain local autonomy over local *sales tax* rates, but eliminate autonomy over local *use tax* rates. Local jurisdictions would receive revenues from taxes on sales by local merchants but depend on sharing of revenues from the statewide local use tax. This arrangement would allow local jurisdictions to meet their obligations under debt covenants that dedicate revenues from local sales tax to debt service. Local governments imposing sales tax rates well below the statewide local use tax rate might compensate local residents for excess use tax on remote purchases. Where local sales tax rates exceed the statewide use tax rate, discrimination against local merchants would remain.

UNALLOCABLE SALES

Proposal D. Remote sales that cannot be allocated to a state (because remote vendors do not know the location of a buyer of digitized content) and remote sales that fall below the *de minimis* threshold (see below) would be subject to a national "substitute" use tax, revenues from which would be shared among the states, perhaps on the basis of estimated consumer spending in the state.[56]

It is not satisfactory to attribute unallocable sales to the state of origin of remote commerce; doing so creates an incentive to locate operations in states with no sales tax. Billing addresses can be used to determine the location of some customers but not all. The need for the national substitute use tax is one advantage of having a nationally uniform state sales tax base, which would be used as the base of that tax. States that have no sales tax (or rates well below the national tax) could refund the national tax (or the difference in rates) to their residents. Technological developments may make this provision unnecessary.

ADMINISTRATIVE ASPECTS

Administration of state sales and use taxes should be simpler and more uniform throughout the nation. Two options deserve attention.

---

56. The substitute use tax would be implemented by the states, not the federal government. In the text, the word "among" thus replaces "with," which might give the impression that the substitute use tax would be imposed by the federal government.

Proposal E1: The Base State Approach.   Taxpayers would collect use tax in all states where sales exceed *de minimis* amounts. But they would file a single form to register in all states and another to pay tax due in all states. Forms might be filed in the state in which the firm has its commercial domicile (the "base state") or with a multistate agency. The base state or multistate agency would forward revenues to states where sales occur, which would divide revenues among local jurisdictions on the basis of information provided by taxpayers. There would be joint audits on behalf of all states and a common appeals process.

Tax authorities in each state would need to know the tax laws of all other states. This system would thus work best if there were a common definition of the tax base. It would not work in the absence of a common menu of potentially taxable products.

Proposal E2: Use of Trusted Third Parties.   This approach would shift compliance from the vendor to a trusted third party (TTP). The TTP would calculate tax and remit it to states where sales are made, with an indication of the division of revenues among local jurisdictions.

Further analysis is needed to determine whether the base-state approach or the TTP approach is more promising.

ZERO-COST COMPLIANCE

Proposal F.   Implementation of a destination-based sales tax requires remote vendors or TTPs to use sophisticated and expensive software. State governments should provide the software at no cost. (There is precedent. When Canada introduced the VAT it subsidized the purchase of new cash registers.) Under the base state approach vendors' discounts should be set to defray costs of compliance. (They might not be needed under the TTP approach.) These costs can be quite high, as a percentage of revenues, for small vendors.

Proposal G. It may be desirable to have a *de minimis* rule; vendors with total remote sales below a certain level would be relieved of the need to participate in the base state system or utilize a TTP.

From an economic point of view, making sales in a state, rather than a physical presence, should be the test of nexus. Yet it may be unreasonable or uneconomical to require firms with small remote sales to participate in the regular system. (There might be relatively little need for a *de minimis* rule if all the primary proposals made here were adopted.)

Concluding Remarks

Because the proposals made here form a package, comments on the entire package are appropriate.

THE INTEGRITY OF THE PROPOSALS

Taken together the primary proposals would radically simplify state sales and use taxes and make it reasonable to impose an expanded duty to collect use tax. If proposed changes are omitted or replaced by the fallback positions, there would be substantially less simplification—so much less that an expanded duty to collect might become questionable.

If there were a menu of taxable products, instead of a uniform and comprehensive base, the software needed to implement use taxes would be more complicated and expensive, classification of products would be more controversial and onerous, state certification of software and a "hold harmless" provision would be problematic, the base state approach and use of TTPs might be infeasible, and the *de minimis* threshold would need to be higher. The severity of problems would depend on the level of aggregation of the menu. Moreover, it is unlikely that technological neutrality would be maintained in constructing the menu. If there were not even a uniform menu from which states would choose their tax base, it seems unlikely that enough simplification could be achieved to justify an expanded duty to collect.

THE QUESTION OF STATE SOVEREIGNTY AND LOCAL AUTONOMY

Some of these proposals (e.g., the proposal for a uniform tax base) may be attacked as an unwelcome intrusion on state fiscal sovereignty. That view loses sight of the larger picture. The state sovereignty that was possible when local merchants sold primarily tangible products almost exclusively to local customers is no longer possible, or at least not a realistic alternative, as it implies enormous complexity for remote vendors and thus the legal inability to tax remote sales, including those in electronic commerce. The proposals represent an attempt to craft a compromise between the need for revenue and the power to set state tax rates—arguably higher orders of state sovereignty—and control over the tax base, arguably a less important aspect of sovereignty. They also attempt to retain local autonomy over local sales and use tax rates.

THE NEED FOR FEDERAL LEGISLATION

In theory it might be possible for the states cooperatively to implement a system such as that proposed here, without federal legislation. If they did, the Supreme Court might eliminate the physical presence test of nexus. In fact, history does not inspire confidence that the states would act in this way, and the Court might not respond as predicted even if they did. In any event, there would be unacceptable uncertainty. Thus it seems almost certain that federal legislation would be required to implement the proposals made here. Rather than requiring that states adopt the proposals (the "stick" approach), legislation could allow an expanded duty to collect only for states that adopt the proposals (the "carrot" approach).

Seizing the Moment for Fundamental Sales Tax Reform

Electronic commerce is eliminating familiar boundaries: between political jurisdictions (between states and between nations), between types of products (goods and services), between industries (telecommunications, cable, satellite, and Internet), and between forms of income (business income, income from services, and royalties). Although the web causes disintermediation (for example, as manufacturers use the power of the Internet to sell directly to consumers), reintermediation is also occurring, as companies spring up to help sift and digest the incredible amount of information that is becoming available on-line and refer customers to one another. Business structures are evolving, as established firms create e-commerce subsidiaries, in part to avoid the duty to collect use tax, and form alliances with uniquely web-based firms (e.g., web browsers, search engines, and Internet service providers).

These and similar developments—and still others that cannot yet be imagined—are placing enormous pressures on traditional institutions and practices of taxation. Sales and income tax systems that were created during the industrial age are, in many ways, not suited to the digital age; this is especially true of the sales and use tax, the topic of these concluding remarks. Having been enacted with little attention to their structure, economic effects, or administration, sales and use taxes have long cried out for reform. Because of the advent of electronic commerce, the time is ripe to respond to those cries by undertaking fundamental reform that produces a rational sales tax system.

Assessing Blame: Foot-Draggers in the State Capitols

Attempts to modify state sales and use taxes encounter a variety of obstacles, including political opposition from some participants in e-commerce and their advocates, who prefer to keep e-commerce a tax-free zone, and foot-dragging from those who would like to tax electronic commerce but seem not to realize that the only way to achieve this objective is to undertake wholesale reform and simplification. The foot-draggers may be the worst enemies of fair and equal taxation. As long as the sales and use tax is so complicated, the Supreme Court almost certainly will not condone taxation of remote commerce, including electronic commerce, and neither Congress nor the Supreme Court will overturn *Quill*—nor should they. Massive simplification is required if remote vendors are to have an expanded duty to collect.

"Technological solutions" alone will not suffice; throwing computers at an incredibly complicated system to "simplify" compliance is like adding more epicycles to a Ptolemaic view of the solar system. The NGA proposal for a voluntary system of compliance based on the use of trusted third parties would not solve the problem. It would reduce the costs borne by vendors in part by transferring them to the states, rather than cutting those costs drastically, which can be done only by reforming and simplifying the system along the lines I have proposed. The key to unraveling the whole mess—the analog of putting the sun in the center of the solar system—is to simplify the sales and use tax system along the lines suggested in the second part of this chapter.

Some argue that it is premature to extend the sales tax to electronic commerce—that we should be patient because of the development of new business structures and practices. Subject to a caveat to be mentioned shortly, that is exactly wrong. True, it would be premature—or downright unwise—to extend the existing sales and use tax to transactions occurring under the new structures. All kinds of business-to-business transactions might improperly be subject to tax, and the need to deal with unsettled issues means that litigation and complexity would abound. But there will never be a good time to apply existing sales and use taxes to these transactions. These new ways of doing business cry out for the type of rational system described in the second part of this chapter. *All transactions between businesses should be exempt.* Only sales to consumers—and essentially all those—should be taxed, no matter how they are conducted. Those are relatively simple rules to implement. With them taxation of all remote commerce, perhaps even by local governments at rates they choose, would be feasible.

There is one caveat to the conclusions stated above. Given the potential of Internet buyers to hide their location, imposing a duty to collect use tax could place domestic vendors of digital content at a competitive disadvantage relative to foreign vendors, especially in tax havens. This risk deserves further consideration but cannot be discussed adequately here.

The Need for an Implicit Moratorium on Taxation of Electronic Commerce

For the next few years electronic commerce that crosses state lines should not be subject to sales and use tax; as the Supreme Court recognized in *Quill*, the system is so complicated that imposing it on remote vendors of any kind would create an unacceptable burden on interstate commerce. But Congress need do nothing to effect a moratorium; absent federal legislation, the legal status quo, as defined by *Quill*, will continue, and remote commerce will, in effect, be exempt, except where nexus exists under *Quill*.[57]

There is actually no practical alternative to some kind of mor-

---

57. Reliance on *Quill* would not produce a moratorium for e-commerce vendors who have nexus in a state where they make sales. That would require passage of state laws.

atorium, given the time that would be required to craft a satisfactory sales tax policy and enact it in enough states to provide convincing evidence that a satisfactory degree of simplification has been achieved. Continuation of the status quo—and the growing revenue loss it would entail—would place pressure on the states to get their house in order by enacting sales and use taxes that are essentially uniform and thus simpler. At the same time, the oft-mentioned existence of state budget surpluses provides the breathing room needed to avoid rushing into ill-advised changes.

The ACEC should not recommend an explicit moratorium on taxation of electronic commerce.[58] A legislated moratorium could cause enormous mischief. For example, it might unduly expand the nexus protection of *Quill;*[59] if poorly crafted, it might provide a temporary exemption for commerce that is electronic only in form; worst of all, the legislative process might convert a proposal for a temporary moratorium into a permanent exemption.

There is no need to specify how long the implicit moratorium should remain in place; it will—and should—be in effect until the states unify their systems. It would probably be worthwhile for the ACEC to advise Congress to revisit the issue, say in three to five years, if it appears that the states have made adequate progress in simplification. If the states have effectively unified their systems, they may be able to convince Congress to override *Quill;* they may even be able to win a case in the Supreme Court. If they have not, they should not achieve victory in either venue.

This strategy involves some risk. If electronic commerce devel-

58. Extension of the moratorium provided by the Internet Tax Freedom Act would have no effect on electronic commerce, aside from Internet access.

59. Dean Andal, a member of the ACEC, has proposed a codification of nexus rules that would expand those in *Quill*. For example, it would substitute "substantial physical presence" for the "physical presence" test of *Quill* and would apply the same nexus rules to income taxes. The Andal proposal is available at www.ecommerccommission.org.

ops without the need to collect use tax, it will not be easy politically to impose a duty to collect, no matter how simple compliance becomes. But, as noted above, there is no alternative, as it would be unconscionable—as well as legally and legislatively unlikely—to impose the present complicated system of sales and use taxes on electronic commerce. This means that the states must act with deliberate haste to reform and simplify their systems. As Governor Leavitt might say, "We are now operating on Internet time and should act like it."

Appendix: Appeal for Fair and Equal Taxation of Electronic Commerce

We the undersigned academic specialists in tax policy, having no direct interest in the outcome of the deliberations of the Advisory Commission on Electronic Commerce, are concerned that the Commission may make recommendations for the tax treatment of electronic commerce that are contrary to the public interest. We therefore respectfully suggest that any recommendations the Commission makes regarding the sales and use tax should satisfy all four of the following general principles, which are consistent with a variety of specific proposals:

1. Electronic commerce should not permanently be treated differently from other commerce. There is no principled reason for a permanent exemption for electronic commerce. Electronic commerce should be taxed neither more nor less heavily than other commerce.

2. Remote sales, including electronic commerce, should, to the extent possible, be taxed by the state of destination of sales, regardless of whether the vendor has a physical presence in the state. In limited cases, where it is impossible to determine the destination of sales of digital content to households, it may be necessary to substitute a surrogate system. In no case should taxation of remote commerce or electronic commerce be limited to origin-

based taxation, which would induce a "race to the bottom" and, in effect, no taxation at all.

3. There must be enough simplification of sales and use taxes to make destination-based taxation of sales feasible. Such simplification might include, for example, unification of the tax bases across states, unification of tax rates within states, and/or sourcing of sales only to the state level, as well as simplification of administrative procedures.

4. A means must be found to eliminate burdens of compliance on sellers making only small amounts of sales in a state. These might include software-based systems made available at state expense, more realistic vendor discounts, and/or *de minimis* rules.

(The statement does not represent the position of the institutions with which the signatories are associated.)

Name	Affiliation
Henry Aaron	Brookings Institution; Assistant Secretary for Planning and Evaluation, Department of Health, Education and Welfare, 1977–78
James Alm	Andrew Young School of Policy Studies, Georgia State University
Rosanne Altshuler	Rutgers University
John E. Anderson	University of Nebraska
Ashish Arora	Carnegie Mellon University
Alan Auerbach	University of California, Berkeley; Deputy Chief of Staff, U.S. Joint Committee on Taxation, 1992
Hugh J. Ault	Boston College Law School
Reuven S. Avi-Yonah	Harvard Law School
Dave Babbel	Wharton School; University of Pennsylvania
Roy Bahl	Andrew Young School of Policy Studies, Georgia State University
Charles L. Ballard	Michigan State University
Marion S. Beaumont	California State University, Long Beach
Robert Berne	New York University

Name	Affiliation
B. Douglas Bernheim	Stanford University
Marsha Blumenthal	University of St. Thomas
William T. Bogart	Case Western Reserve University
John H. Bowman	Virginia Commonwealth University
David F. Bradford	Woodrow Wilson School, Princeton University, and New York University School of Law; Deputy Assistant Secretary of the Treasury for Tax Analysis, 1975–1976; Member of the President's Council of Economic Advisers, 1991–93
George F. Break	University of California, Berkeley, emeritus
David A. Brennen	University of Richmond Law School
Evelyn Brody	Chicago-Kent College of Law
Jeffrey R. Brown	Harvard University, Kennedy School of Government
Lawrence R. Brown	Lewis & Clark College, School of Law
Neil Bruce	University of Washington
Paul L. Caron	University of Cincinnati College of Law
Karl E. Case	Wellesley College
Howard Chernick	Hunter College, City University of New York
Robert Chirinko	Emory University
Charles Clotfelter	Duke University
Julie H. Collins	University of North Carolina - Chapel Hill, Kenan-Flager Business School
Joseph J. Cordes	George Washington University
Gary Cornia	Brigham Young University
Paul Courant	University of Michigan
Steven G. Craig	University of Houston
Julie Berry Cullen	University of Michigan
Martin David	University of Wisconsin
Charles de Bartolome	University of Colorado at Boulder
Larry DeBoer	Purdue University
Peter Diamond	Massachusetts Institute of Technology
Joseph Dodge	University of Texas Law School
Thomas Downes	Tufts University

Name	Affiliation
John F. Due	University of Illinois, Urbana-Champaign, emeritus
William Dumcombe	Syracuse University
Amy Dunbar	University of Connecticut
Richard Dye	Lake Forest College
Robert Ebel	World Bank
Kelly D. Edmiston	Andrew Young School of Policy Studies, Georgia State University
Daniel Feenberg	National Bureau of Economic Research
Alan L. Feld	Boston University
Glen W. Fisher	Wichita State University, emeritus
Ronald Fisher	Michigan State University
William F. Fox	University of Tennessee
Martin L. Fried	Syracuse University College of Law
Don Fullerton	University of Texas; Deputy Assistant Secretary of the Treasury for Tax Analysis, 1985–87
William Gale	Brookings Institution
Greg Geisler	Georgia State University
William M. Gentry	Columbia University
Wendy Gerzog	University of Baltimore School of Law
J. Fred Giertz	University of Illinois at Urbana-Champaign
Malcolm Gillis	President, Rice University
Tim Goodspeed	Hunter College, City University of New York
Austan Goolsbee	University of Chicago
Robert H. Gordon	University of Michigan
Larry Goulder	Stanford University
Michael Graetz	Yale Law School; Deputy Asst. Secretary of the Treasury for Tax Policy, 1990–92
Kenneth V. Greene	State University of New York, Binghamton
Jonathan Gruber	Massachusetts Institute of Technology
Sanjay Gupta	Arizona State University
Daniel Halperin	Harvard Law School; Deputy Assistant Secretary of the Treasury for Tax Policy, 1978–81
Arnold C. Harberger	University of California, Los Angeles

Name	Affiliation
Joseph E. Harrington Jr.	The Johns Hopkins University
C. Lowell Harriss	Columbia University, emeritus
Robert Haveman	University of Wisconsin, Madison
Richard Hawkins	University of West Florida
Walter Hellerstein	University of Georgia Law School
W. Bartley Hildreth	Wichita State University
Douglas Holtz-Eakin	Syracuse University
Scott Houser	California State University, Fresno
Glenn Hubbard	Columbia University; Deputy Assistant Secretary of the Treasury for Trade and Investment Policy, 1977–80
David Hudson	University of Florida College of Law
Gary Hufbauer	International Institute of Economics; Deputy Assistant Secretary of the Treasury for Trade and Investment Policy, 1977–80
John M. Huie	Purdue University
Robert P. Inman	Wharton School, University of Pennsylvania
Calvin Johnson	University of Texas Law School
William R. Johnson	University of Virginia
Kenneth Judd	Hoover Institution, Stanford University
Richard L. Kaplan	University of Illinois College of Law
Daphne A. Kenyon	Simmons College
Marjorie E. Kornhauser	Tulane Law School
Laurence Kotlikoff	Boston University
Helen F. Ladd	Duke University
Michael B. Lang	University of Southern Maine
Jane H. Leuthold	University of Illinois at Urbana-Champaign
Arik Levinson	Univeristy of Wisconsin, Madison
Henry J. Lischer Jr.	Southern Methodist University Law School
Andrew B. Lyon	University of Maryland
Louis J. Maccini	The Johns Hopkins University
Brigitte Madrian	University of Chicago
Jorge Martinez	Andrew Young School of Policy Studies, Georgia State University
Michael J. McIntyre	Wayne State University Law School

Name	Affiliation
Charles McLure	Hoover Institution, Stanford University; Deputy Assistant Secretary of the Treasury for Tax Analysis, 1983–85
Martin J. McMahon Jr.	University of Florida, Frederic G. Levin College of Law
Gilbert E. Metcalf	Tufts University
Bruce D. Meyer	Northwestern University
Peter Mieszkowski	Rice University
John L. Mikesell	Indiana University-Bloomington
Lillian F. Mills	University of Arizona
Robert A. Moffitt	The Johns Hopkins University
George Mundstock	University of Miami Law School
Alicia H. Munnell	Boston College; Assistant Secretary of the Treasury for Economic Policy, 1993–95; Member of the President's Council of Economic Advisers, 1995–97
Matthew N. Murray	University of Tennessee, Knoxville
Peggy Musgrave	University of California-Santa Cruz
Richard A. Musgrave	Harvard University, emeritus
Dick Netzer	New York University
Sarah E. Nutter	George Mason University
William Oakland	Tulane University
Wallace Oates	University of Maryland
Oliver Oldman	Harvard Law School
Edgar O. Olsen	University of Virginia
James A. Papke	Purdue University
Ronald A. Pearlman	Georgetown University Law Center; Deputy Assistant Secretary of the Treasury for Tax Policy, 1983–84; Assistant Secretary of the Treasury for Tax Policy, 1984–85; Chief of Staff of the Joint Committee on Taxation, 1988–90
John M. Peha	Carnegie Mellon University
Robert J. Peroni	George Washington University
George A. Plesko	Sloan School of Management, Massachusetts Institute of Technology

Name	Affiliation
Thomas F. Pogue	University of Iowa
Clarissa Potter	Georgetown University Law Center
Elizabeth Powers	University of Illinois
Antonio Rangel	Stanford University
Andrew Reschovsky	University of Wisconsin-Madison
James A. Richardson	Louisiana State University
Raymond J. Ring Jr.	University of South Dakota
Mildred W. Robinson	University of Virginia School of Law
Diane Lim Rogers	Urban Institute
Paul Romer	Graduate School of Business and Hoover Institution, Stanford University
Michael Rothschild	Woodrow Wilson School, Princeton University
Daniel L. Rubinfeld	University of California, Berkeley
Allan Samansky	Ohio State University College of Law
Andrew A. Samwick	Dartmouth College
Ferdinand P. Schoettle	University of Minnesota Law School
John Karl Scholz	University of Wisconsin, Madison; Deputy Assistant Secretary of the Treasury for Tax Analysis, 1997–98
Robert M. Schwab	University of Maryland
Amy Ellen Schwartz	New York University
W. Eugene Seago	Virginia Tech
Bruce A. Seaman	Georgia State University
Laurence Seidman	University of Delaware
Douglas Shackelford	University of North Carolina
Daniel N. Shaviro	NYU Law School
Steve Sheffrin	University of California-Davis
Reed Shuldiner	University of Pennsylvania Law School
Todd Sinai	The Wharton School, University of Pennsylvania
David Sjoquist	Andrew Young School of Policy Studies, Georgia State University
Jonathan Skinner	Dartmouth College
Paul Smoke	Massachusetts Institute of Technology
Jon Sonstelle	University of California, Santa Barbara

Name	Affiliation
Janet F. Speyrer	University of New Orleans
Eugene Steuerle	Urban Institute; Deputy Assistant Secretary of the Treasury for Tax Analysis, 1987–89
Leanna Stiefel	New York University
Robert Strauss	Carnegie-Mellon University
Corrine Taylor	Wellesley College
Eric Toder	Urban Institute; Deputy Assistant Secretary of the Treasury for Tax Analysis, 1993–96
William J. Turnier	University of North Carolina School of Law
Holley Ulbrich	Strom Thurmond Institute, Clemson University
Stephen Vasek	University of Kentucky, College of Law
Sally Wallace	Andrew Young School of Policy Studies, Georgia State University
Lawrence Walters	Brigham Young University
Rob Wassmer	California State University—Sacramento
Michael Wasylenko	Syracuse University
David A. Weisbach	University of Chicago Law School
Ann Dryden Witte	Wellesley College
John Witte	University of Wisconsin, Madison
Bernard Wolfman	Harvard Law School
George K. Yin	University of Virginia
George Zodrow	Rice University
C. Kurt Zorn	Indiana University-Bloomington

Margaret Jane Radin

3

Retooling Contract
for the Digital Era

$\mathbf{T}$he advent of electronic commerce in the global networked environment is creating a crisis for contract, the legal institution of enforceable exchange transactions. In the midst of this crisis, it is important to begin with the understanding that technology itself will not solve the crisis by doing away with the need for law.

At least in the United States, it is widely believed that "private ordering" of economic activity works better than government "regulation" of such activity. It may be less widely recognized, however, that private ordering cannot function without a legal infrastructure, which itself is a form of governmental structuring of economic activity. Private ordering is supposed to function through voluntary exchange between private actors. At minimum what is needed for such exchanges to take place in an orderly manner are a fairly stable set of entitlements (a property system) and a fairly stable set of rules of exchange (a contract system). These systems of legal rules form the infrastructure that is requisite for a market order. Technology does not render these requisites obsolete.

Some people argue that actors should be able to make whatever deals they like, period, without benefit of a legal oversight system. They argue that technology renders such "private" deals possible as never before. But the problem comes over the issue of enforcement. If the only enforcement is self-help, whether it is technological self-help or some other kind, then we have anarchy, not law.

When it comes to contracts, anarchy will not suffice. We still need law, for three reasons. First, we continue to believe that certain deals should be enforced through orderly and peaceful means, even if one party wants to renege (and even if that party uses technology to renege). Second, we continue to recognize that certain purported deals should not be enforced because they are not deals at all—because they have been arrived at by force or fraud or entered into by children and so on. Third, at least in developed legal systems, we continue to recognize public policy limits on private deal making. Even some deals that have been voluntarily entered into by the parties should not be enforced. Sale of children or slave labor are the easy cases, but the hard cases must continue to be the subject of public policy debates (perhaps in the digital era personal privacy is one of them).

These limitations on contract require a legal infrastructure as the policing mechanism to separate the valid contracts from the invalid. Moreover, the legal infrastructure must meet the conditions traditionally known as the *rule of law:* the rules must be reasonably stable and known to the actors, and the actors must be able to conform their behavior to them. Some would say in addition that the rules must conform to minimum notions of due process and evenhandedness.

The fact that legal infrastructure is necessary does not mean that all of the needed infrastructure must be exclusively promulgated by the traditional institutional structure known as the nation-state. Instead, a mix of institutional backing is possible and likely. Some portions of the necessary market infrastructure could be promulgated by a different institution that had the support of the economic actors involved. Some portions could arise by custom as long as those who adhered to the custom were able to keep it as robust as it needs to be for a market to flourish. Determining which institutions are best for which aspects of the needed infrastructure is part of what we need to do to work our way through the crisis caused by the transition to global electronic commerce. Customary systems will often be unsuited for complex market functions because they tend to work best among close-knit groups and because their main enforcement mechanism is exclusion.

However the institutional structures are sorted out, a legal infrastructure for contract is badly needed to get the era of electronic commerce off the ground. To date, industry leaders, governmental leaders, and academics have debated encryption policy, copyright, trademark, privacy, and database protection much more than they have considered the future of contract. Yet if contracts purporting to alter property rights and privacy rights become ubiquitous in the digital environment, then the background rules of intellectual property and privacy rights will fade in importance. Instead, we will be arguing whether the contracts altering them are valid and enforceable. The important questions will involve the rules structuring the institution of contract.

The fact that the advent of e-commerce creates a crisis for contract does not mean that the problems are insoluble or that e-commerce must flounder in anarchy. Nor does the crisis mean, necessarily, that the problems cannot be solved by evolutionary rather than revolutionary means—adaptating and reshaping existing legal doctrines and institutions rather than jettisoning them and fashioning new ones. Probably it will turn out that some new rules and institutions are needed, but that the many of the old ones can be adapted quite satisfactorily.

What the crisis does mean, though, is that industry leaders and others interested in promoting the advent of global e-commerce should focus on the need for a legal infrastructure for contract and should work together with governments and others to develop that infrastructure. In this sense, the crisis in the institution of contract is in fact a unique opportunity for business to help structure the environment in which it must operate in the future.

In this chapter, I provide background for the process of developing the contractual infrastructure for e-commerce. In order to do so, the chapter will focus on five interrelated problems for contract that are created (or greatly exacerbated) by the networked digital environment:

1. Authentication: How do we know who made a particular deal and what will count as a definitive record of its terms?

2. Binding commitment: How will interactions between people and computers create binding commitments? In particular, how should we think about
   • Click-wrap contracts?
   • Machine-to-machine contracts?
   • Contracts in which distributors pass obligations on to everyone in a distribution chain?

3. Standardization: Will uniform standardized "adhesion" contracts be enforceable?

4. Excluded terms: Under what circumstances should particular terms in e-commerce deals be disallowed?

5. Jurisdiction and choice of law: Whatever the governing

rules of choice of law and jurisdiction would otherwise be, can they be routinely altered by contract?

Authentication

Of the five problems constituting the crisis in contract, the issue of authentication has received the most notice. The practical issue for any deal for which enforcement is sought after the fact, when someone is trying to repudiate, is the need to pin down the operative facts about the deal: that a deal was actually made, and that it involved particular parties and particular terms (Harry Hansen from Mountain View, not Harry Hansen from Menlo Park; for a price of $1,200, not $12,000). The English statute of frauds required that contracts for the sale of land or for sale of goods over a certain amount would be invalid unless in writing, signed, and sealed (bearing the imprint of a seal). The seal requirement gradually fell away, but the statute of frauds still exists (although it varies slightly from place to place), so a great many contracts must be in writing and signed by the parties in order to be valid.

What will count as a writing in the digital era? (Is an e-mail a writing? Is a click in a box on the screen labeled "I accept" a writing?) What will count as a signature? (The sig in my e-mail?) Because these problems have been noticed, technological digital signature schemes and other methods of electronic authentication are being and have been developed. These electronic authentication schemes function, among other things, to enable on-line contracting by granting legal significance to digital signatures in situations where physical signatures would otherwise be required.

Digital signatures are being legally implemented in many places. Unfortunately, the emerging legal implementation schemes are nonuniform. Under the European Union (EU) digital signature directive, various different national regimes are developing. In the

United States, many jurisdictions have enacted or are considering some kind of legislation relating to electronic authentication, but so far this is a patchwork.[1]

Some of the new laws are technology-specific, calling for public key cryptography, and others are technology-neutral, providing for authentication however achieved. Technology-specific laws pose two policy issues: (1) they are often outdated before the enactment process is finished; (2) the favored technology enjoys something like a government-sanctioned monopoly. Technology-neutral laws, on the other hand, may be more difficult to draft efficaciously because the tendency is to make them vague and general.

With respect to technology-specific laws that involve public key cryptography in particular, many questions remain open with respect to implementation of a public key infrastructure system with certificate authorities (CAs): how CAs should be authorized, what types of liabilities they should bear, and so on. On these topics many detailed questions arise: What can businesses do to protect themselves against fraudulent digital signatures? Can a defrauded party seek indemnity from the CA who guaranteed the defective signature? What levels of proof must a CA require before it issues a certificate? Will a CA be liable to a defrauded party if it fails to require adequate proof? Will a CA be immune from liability if it does require adequate proof? If CAs are immune, will liability be thrown back to the defrauded party who mistakenly relied on a certificate? Can a CA disclaim liability?

---

1. Federal legislation dealing with digital signatures is pending. The proposed Uniform Electronic Transactions Act (UETA), which has some provisions bearing on electronic authentication, has been enacted in California and is being presented to other state legislatures. A useful catalog of digital signature legislation is at the web site of the Chicago firm of McBride Baker & Coles, http://www.mbc.com/ds_sum.html.

Binding Commitment:
The Problem of Contract Formation

A threshold issue in any contractual dispute is contract formation (i.e., whether or not the parties entered into a binding contract). The issue of what will make a purported contract binding in cyberspace is basic to electronic commerce. Traditionally, people picture contracts as involving a meeting of the minds or autonomous consent between two human parties. The traditional picture does not describe much of contemporary commercial practice off-line, yet we are probably not ready to relinquish the notion of consent entirely. In e-commerce the interaction that is the basis of contract is an aspect of the computer/human interface, rather than an aspect of communication between humans. It remains to be seen how the tension between the traditional picture and the necessities of commercial practice will play out in the transactional aspects of the computer/human interface.

To explore the emerging issues involving contract formation in the digital environment, I outline three methods of contract formation in electronic commerce. To begin thinking about how the legal system might treat these kinds of contracts, I compare them with their precursors in the off-line world. I call the three methods of contract formation *click-wrap*, *machine-made*, and *viral* contracting. In each case, the procedure deviates from the traditional picture of contract. For that reason, some observers (those who have trouble characterizing the procedure as an instance of consent by the recipient) will find each procedure problematic for contract formation, especially with respect to enforcement of terms that seem unusual and adverse to the user.

"Click-Wrap" Contracts

If you go to Disney.com, "where the magic lives online," you may (or may not) scroll down to and read this small print at the bottom of the home page: "Please click here for legal restrictions and terms of use applicable to this site. Use of this site signifies your agreement to the terms of use."

If you do click there, you will find a lot of fine print:

> By uploading materials to any Forum or submitting any materials to us, you automatically grant (or warrant that the owner of such rights has expressly granted) us a perpetual, royaltyfree, irrevocable, nonexclusive right and license to use, reproduce, modify, adapt, publish, translate, create derivative works from, and distribute such materials or incorporate such materials into any form, medium, or technology now known or later developed throughout the universe. In addition, you warrant that all so-called moral rights in those materials have been waived. . . .
>
> You agree that any action at law or in equity arising out of or relating to these terms shall be filed only in the state or federal courts located in Los Angeles County and you hereby consent and submit to the personal jurisdiction of such courts for the purposes of litigating any such action.

Countless other web sites have internal pages of fine print of their own. There are enough of them to have spawned a couple of acronyms—TOS (terms of service) and COU (conditions of use). What is the user bound to by reason of having some kind of interaction with such a site? There is every reason to believe that all commercial web sites will use a TOS or COU of this kind. Right now, each TOS or COU seems to be individually drafted. Perhaps in the future, as I discuss later, industries may settle on standardized sets of terms.

Precursors of Click-Wrap Contracts

Web site presentation of terms is analogous in certain significant respects to what is known as a *shrink-wrap license*, usually used in software distribution. Roughly speaking, there are two different kinds of shrink-wrap licenses, depending on whether the terms are presented before or after the purchase of the software. In the first kind, the software box is covered by plastic shrink-wrap, and the terms are printed on the shrink-wrap so you can see the terms before purchase; they inform you that if you break the shrink-wrap you have agreed to the terms. The second kind of shrink-wrap license (which gets its name only by its association with the first kind), informs you on the outside of the box that there are terms inside that you will see later (perhaps on the screen when you run the software) and that you will be bound to them if you use the software.

The legal validity of shrink-wrap licenses—that is, whether or not presentation of terms in this way causes a contract to be formed—is still in doubt. One well-known case validating the second kind of shrink-wrap license was *ProCD v. Zeidenberg*.[2] In that case, ProCD's product was a CD containing a telephone number database. A purported contract that appeared on the screen when the CD was read stated that users could not copy the database. If valid, this was a contractual extension of ProCD's rights under copyright law since, under U.S. copyright law, databases are not protected if they are "unoriginal."[3] Zeidenberg, the defendant, relied on copyright law to copy the database; ProCD relied on contract law to argue that he couldn't. Judge Frank Easterbrook sided with ProCD.

2. 86 F.3d 1337 (7th Cir. 1997).
3. As far as federal copyright law is concerned, unoriginal databases are in the public domain. Legislation is pending that would supplement copyright by granting independent protection to databases.

On the issue of contract formation, given that the terms weren't seen by the buyer before he purchased the product, Judge Easterbrook held that the contract was validly formed as long as something on the outside of the box warned the consumer that terms were inside, and as long as the consumer could return the product for a refund after viewing the additional terms. *ProCD* has proved to be an influential case—though perhaps more for its holding that the contract was not preempted by federal law (discussed below) than for its holding on contract formation. Nevertheless, another judge might have held otherwise with respect to contract information; another judge in another jurisdiction might still hold otherwise.

A web site that shows you the terms and says, "If you click in this box you have agreed to the terms," is somewhat analogous to the first kind of shrink-wrap license. The web site is programmed so that you won't get to use the site if you don't click in the box; similarly, you won't get to use shrink-wrapped software if you don't break the shrink-wrap. The analogy is not perfect. It may be easier to read terms that are presented to you on your computer screen than to read the terms on a shrink-wrapped package while you are in the store. Also, of course, it would be easier to keep a copy of the web site terms because you could copy them to your hard drive or print them out.

Some web sites say on their home page nothing more than "Terms of Use"; Beyond.com, a purveyor of software, is a prominent example. Such a message may be interpreted as saying to the user, "By continuing to use this site you are bound to a set of terms which you will only see if you choose to click on them." This is somewhat analogous to the second kind of shrink-wrap contract, in which you are bound to further terms inside the box (or on the first screen). The fact that many home pages do not tell you explicitly that there are binding terms inside is a disanalogy, as is the fact that in the software situation it is usually the case that the terms show themselves to you, whereas in the web site case you must *do* something in order to see them. When a process like this has been held to form a contract, it has usually been required that the user be able to unwind the deal after viewing the terms (i.e., by returning the product for a refund). Therefore, another disanalogy may be that it is difficult for the consumer to return the product after viewing the terms.[4]

There are other contracts in the off-line world in which the buyer doesn't see many of the terms until after buying the product. We purchase tickets, tour packages, and countless other items (including shrink-wrapped software) over the phone before we see the fine print. Consumer product warranties are often inside the box. In some classes of these contracts, such as the fine-print inserts that occasionally come with my credit card bill, new terms are imposed at the seller's will. In all these contracts, the promisor must at least be given the option of declining after the fact, by unwinding his or her initial acceptance of the product (e.g., ceasing to use the credit card). The option in practice, however, is usually only theoretically possible. I'm unlikely to return my tour package after I've planned my vacation; I've never packed up something I bought over the phone because I didn't like the fine print on the back of the invoice when it came.

In the United States, the Uniform Commercial Code, separately enacted by each state, is the primary legislation governing many contracts for the sale of tangible goods. The main impetus for the proposed Article 2B of the Uniform Commercial Code was to add information licensing transactions so as to validate shrink-wrap licenses. The proposed legislation became extremely controversial primarily because of shrink-wrap validation and other expansions of licensors' rights at the expense of licensees' (the American Law

4. For example, a group of Linux users who did not wish to purchase or use the Windows license with their computers had a great deal of difficulty trying to return the Windows software. See *Wired News*, http://wired.lycos.com/news/news/technology/story/17926.html.

Institute failed to approve the 2B draft). The proponents did not withdraw it, however, but instead renamed it the Uniform Computer Information Transactions Act (UCITA). The National Commissioners on Uniform State Laws at their July 1999 meeting approved the draft for presentation to state legislatures, and attempts to enact UCITA as the law governing information contracts have recently begun.

Machine-Made Contract

Machine-made contracts as they are now used or foreseen fall into two broad categories: computers as electronic agents and computers as electronic enforcers. In the first category, computers are programmed to "negotiate" and "agree" with one another. In the second, computers are programmed to force on a user whatever terms the programmer chooses.

ELECTRONIC AGENTS

Right now, the electronic agent scenario is most often seen (or foreseen) in industrial procurement and general supply-chain management, which is a burgeoning business and technical field. The vast power of digital automation is being coupled with principles of just-in-time manufacture and distribution. In this form of industrial organization, many repetitive tasks are or will be accomplished by machine, including ordering and paying for supplies that are routinely needed at certain points in a process. The ordering, delivery, and payment for such supplies means that there are contractual terms surrounding the transaction—the time of delivery, what to do if the supplies do not arrive in time or are defective, what to do if the payment is late, and so on, all of which can in principle be largely handled by machine.

Computer programs can "negotiate" and enter into "agreements" with one another. The Secure Socket Layer (SSL) protocol, for example, which your browser uses to establish a secure connection with a web site, selects a method of encryption that works for both. The Platform for Internet Content Selection (PICS) protocol, developed by the World Wide Web Consortium (W3C), enables your computer to determine which privacy policies you are willing to accept from a web site.

Although automated supply-chain management is the harbinger of the form of machine-made contract I've designated *electronic agency*, in the near future these machine-made contracts may well become widespread. It is predicted that "electronic agents" will shop for us and arrange our affairs in many ways.

ELECTRONIC ENFORCERS

In the second category of machine-made contract, now known as *digital rights management systems* or *trusted systems*, computer programs enforce the terms of a transfer of digital content. Such systems can be programmed to prevent delivery of a piece of content until payment is received and credited, to prevent all copying of a piece of content or the making of more than a certain number of copies, to prevent printing a copy or more than a certain number of copies, to prevent reading it more than once or more than a certain number of times, to destroy the content if the user attempts to do something prohibited, and so on. A popular anarchic vision of self-ordering in the digital world tends to assume that all the terms desired by a content distributor will be rendered self-enforcing through the use of technological rights management systems. Such self-enforcement will likely be a significant aspect of the human/computer interface for e-commerce.

Precursors to Machine-Made Contracts

THE ELECTRONIC AGENT SCENARIO

In the first kind of machine-made contract, one firm's machine negotiates and agrees with another firm's machine in an automated procurement process. In a sense this is like a classic "battle of the forms," in which a buyer's purchase order (sent by one human being with authority to bind a firm) has one set of fine print and the seller's invoice (sent by another human being with authority to bind a firm) has another. The legislation attempting to deal with the battle of the forms, UCC 2-207, has been criticized because it is too complex, ambiguous, readily misunderstood, doesn't deal adequately with all the types of cases that arise, and in some scenarios irrationally gives one party all the terms in its form depending on the order in which the forms were sent.

The machine-made contract is significantly disanalogous with the battle of the forms, however, because in the world of machine-made contract the machines can sometimes resolve the battle with more precision. If machine A runs a program that can accept terms L, M, or N, and machine B runs a program that can accept terms N, O, or P, the machines can "agree" to a term (N) that both parties have approved (if running a computer that runs a certain program with this capability counts as having approved it).

The hypothetical situation suggests some difficulties. If machine A accepts L, M, or N and machine B accepts M, N, or O, the programs would need rules for deciding whether to agree to M or N; the machines might need first to agree on those rules. Moreover, a human being might want to agree to M only if N is also agreed to; in general, terms are interdependent because it is the entire set of terms that matters economically. (That is, I might accept a shorter warranty but only if the price is also lowered.) Thus, it is more likely that machine A would be programmed with one or more sets of terms so that it will only do business with machine Bs that are programmed with at least one set of terms in common. This likelihood is one reason to think that standardized sets of terms are likely to be prevalent in the digital world. (I come back later to the topic of standardized terms.)

Some problems arise when considering how a machine is supposed to "know" when human judgment is required. If sets of terms are incompletely standardized, so that machine A with a set of terms M (containing one hundred terms including z) encounters machine B with set of terms M' (containing ninety-nine identical terms but z' instead of z), machine A would not make the deal. But a human might see immediately that the deal should still be made because the choice between z and z' is unimportant. The computer could be programmed to alert a human (let out a beep or put a dialogue box on the screen) in this event. Instead, maybe all sets of terms M, N, and O acceptable to the party responsible for the programmed computer could contain subsets x, x', x'' and z, z', z'' for all terms like z that its programmer knows have variants that might be encountered. Then either all terms the machine encounters that are still not in the program would void the deal or, again, a mechanism for alerting a human would be needed.

Consider the general idea of using programmed computers as acquiring agents. For example, a shopping 'bot might search the web and purchase a rare classical recording I have programmed it to look for. Or, more interestingly, it might purchase a rare classical recording that it has been programmed to "know" is similar to those I already have. This scenario is analogous to employing a personal shopper or an agent to purchase art for my collection. The agent can be empowered to make binding purchases for me without my consenting to each purchase. It will be more difficult to program a computer to make judgments about what will fit in my collection and what won't and how it will "know" when it needs to get my approval on a specific item that might be borderline. The needed kinds of transactional safeguards will be different. Fooling a computer is different from defrauding a human; computers are more easily fooled in many ways. They don't know when you're joking, or when you meant 100 even though you typed 1,000. They are, however, less easily fooled in other ways—they make fewer errors in mathematics, for example. Machines are also less likely to go on frolics of their own.

ELECTRONIC ENFORCERS

Digital rights management systems are harder to analogize to contractual arrangements in the off-line world. Perhaps when it comes to the imposition of terms by a rights management system, we have passed the limits of what we can assimilate to the category of contractual arrangements. Such a system is indeed a faithful "agent" for the purveyor of content because it makes the content available to the user only on the terms it is programmed to enforce. A big difference between this arrangement and a contract, though, is that contracts can be breached. Our system—at least in many contemporary economic interpretations—contemplates breach when it is efficient under the circumstances. Our system also contemplates breach when the user wants to exercise a citizen's right to test the legality of the terms. When legality is tested, the state (on behalf of the community) passes on the acceptability of the terms, creating a check on what kinds of terms can be implemented. Thus, self-enforcement is not the same as enforcement by a court. The analogy to contract seems inapposite; rather, technological management systems are a species of technological self-help, like sending over a committee of one's friends to intimidate a storekeeper into paying a debt.

Of course, the buyer's decision to purchase content under the terms of such a system is itself possibly contractual, in that the buyer is choosing to use such a system and accepts its consequences. Would the analogy then be merely to purchasing a product with certain known benefits and drawbacks? Or perhaps the more appropriate analogy would be to a contract in which the buyer could not purchase the product unless he agreed to waive all his legal rights. Although contracts deviating from the traditional picture of autonomous consent are common in the off-line world, it is hard to think of any contracts in practice in which buyers are held to have entered into such a blanket waiver.

With the advent of these systems, technology has (at least temporarily) outrun the law. People are betting different ways on whether and when the law will catch up. Legal support for trusted systems has been enacted, in the form of the provisions of the Digital Millennium Copyright Act aimed at preventing copy protection and management systems from being disabled. Legislation has not yet had anything to say about the other side of the picture (possible legal limitations on such systems), though there are some rudimentary (and unfortunately ambiguous) limitations in the proposed UCITA. Courts will likely eventually find it necessary to address questions regarding possible limits on the operations of copy protection and management systems, especially if economic circumstances make the information unavailable through other means.

Viral Contracts

Consider contracts whose obligations purport to "run" to successors of immediate parties (i.e., contracts imposed by a transferor that attempt to bind all future transferees in the chain of distribution). These could be called contracts that run with an information object, but I prefer to call them *viral contracts* because they may be expected to go along with viral marketing. (Viral marketing gets your customers to market your product, and they get their customers to do so, and so on.) Many web firms have "affiliate" programs that do this.

Viral contracts are already important in the networked digital environment. An early example is the open source movement for software licensing and development. The principles of this movement include the idea that each recipient in a chain of distribution is bound to make public any improvements effected in the source code. For example, the General Public License promulgated by the Free Software Foundation governs the Linux operating system and other software. This example is a narrowing of copyright (in fact the license is known as *copyleft*).

The same technique can also be used to broaden copyright or other intellectual property entitlement schemes. An example would be a "running" waiver of the fair use defense to copyright infringement, in which a distributor seeks to foreclose that defense for all users in a chain of distribution.

The use of viral contracts will no doubt increase as viral marketing catches on. Affiliate programs are on the rise because they are much easier than referrals in "real" space: just put a link to my web site on your web site and I'll give you 10 percent for every sale that comes from your referral. Both the linking and the necessary tracking for payment are trivial for Internet technology. In the typical affiliate scenario today, the buyer must come to the site of the original seller and will therefore contract with the seller. One can imagine, however, other scenarios in which subsequent parties in the chain of distribution contract with each other but in which the original seller wishes to control the contractual terms.

In particular, software publishers have hitherto licensed rather than sold their software so that they could restrict transfer. In turn they have restricted transfer primarily because of the difficulty of maintaining restrictions on use of the software by holders remote in the distribution chain. Perhaps market forces will bring this total restraint-on-alienation model into disfavor. Perhaps software publishers would much prefer viral sales contracts with running obligations on all transferees in a chain of distribution and merely are in doubt about their enforceability or acceptability against transferees, in which case changes in the law could precipitate an increase in viral contracting.

Precursors to Viral Contracts

The category of terms that are inherited automatically from a predecessor in interest is hard to assimilate to the picture of autonomous consent, at least if those terms are obligations. (There are fewer problems with inheriting benefits.) In any situation in which duties are handed on to successors, one might expect at minimum to see a legally imposed requirement that the successor must take with notice of the duty. That gives the buyer the information needed to decide on his price for the package (i.e., underlying item with duty attached). A buyer would presumably pay less for a computer burdened with a running promise not to run any Unix programs than she would for a computer without such an attached obligation.

For tangible goods UCC 2-210 provides that contractual rights can be assigned in a range of cases. The situation with delegation of duties is less clear, however, because delegation can be prevented by agreement and also by a party who feels justifiably insecure if duties are handed on. Even when delegation of duties is permitted, the delegating party remains liable. The question of automatic delegation of duties down a chain of distribution (rather than a single delegation, with knowledge of the other party) has not arisen because distributors of tangible goods have not normally sought to burden them with running restrictions or obligations.

Viral contracts are basically a new legal phenomenon. I believe we have not seen many cases in the off-line world of attempts to impose restrictions on tangible objects in the form of duties that must be performed by anyone who purchases the object. Indeed, it seems that the only standard situation in which running obligations can be created in the off-line world, absent statutory authorization, are the covenants running with the land and equitable servitudes used in structuring real property entitlements. Notice of the running obligation is the minimum requirement for such land obligations to be valid.

In addition to notice, the common law developed an elaborate set of doctrines that were supposed to act as a check on which schemes of this kind would be enforceable (the obligations must "touch and concern land," for example). The doctrines are notoriously confusing. Putting the best spin on them, they might be understood to operate collectively to screen out contractual schemes that try to enact in a private manner things that would be clearly contrary to public policy or anticompetitive (for example, "whoever owns this house must not rent to non-Caucasians"; "whoever owns this house must buy all groceries at the developer's store").

Obligations that run with land are interestingly similar to standard contracts in that they are typically imposed uniformly on groups of owners in a subdivision or condominium. Analogous contracts in the digital environment are also likely to be imposed on large groups by a promulgating firm. Unlike land obligations, where the extent of obligation to others is known at the outset because the number of affected lots is known, viral contracts in the digital environment may be more problematic because the extent of obligations to others may be unknown. In any case, it is not true that a promise can run with the land to impose obligations on successors just because the original parties say so; notice to successors is needed, as well as something more than that, to police such schemes for acceptability. It will most likely not be true that a promise can run with a digital object to impose obligations on successors just because an original licensor says so.

Standardization

A system of contract is legal infrastructure. Compare it to technical infrastructure, such as the SSL protocol or the SET protocol. By analogy with technical standards, legal standards (i.e., standardized contractual terms) might reduce the transaction costs of the proliferation of different terms and uncertain enforceability. But standards are two-sided. On the one hand, transactions are easier if certain sets of terms are understood by all to govern the transaction. On the other hand, the emergence of standards, whether through the market or by legislation, may sometimes be symptomatic of market failure and is often thought by courts and policymakers to signify oppression rather than efficiency.

One way to get a standard is by legislation (such as UCITA in the United States, if enacted). Another way to get a standard is by industry agreement or industry accession. In fact a legislative standard may come about when industry players want it but cannot agree among themselves. Like Hobbesian cooperators, they might be able to coordinate enough to get the standard imposed on them by the governmental Leviathan, even though in the absence of Leviathan there would be too much incentive for each one to defect. Certainly if workable sets of terms can be standardized, whether by market operation or by legislative fiat, at minimum firms will not have to pay armies of lawyers to think up terms like warranting that "all so-called moral rights" have been waived, and the expectations of both sellers and buyers will be solidified.

Yet it is possible to see, especially from the perspective of public choice theory, that both legislative enactment and private industry agreement (or tacit coordination) can signify rent-seeking, a species of inefficiency (market failure). Powerful market actors often get legislation enacted that favors their profits at the expense of society as a whole. Industry agreements are suspect on cartelization grounds. Hobbesian coordinators could be cordinating on rent-seeking rather than on a reduction of rent-seeking.

In contrast, both legislative enactment and private industry agreement could be efficient. Legislative enactment could indeed represent a reduction of rent-seeking, an efficient solution to a coordination problem, as could private industry agreement. The economic issue—whether a set of uniform terms is efficient or anti-competitive—is indeterminate in the abstract. At least, economically speaking, it is necessary to evaluate such standards in context.

Traditionally courts have looked more favorably on standard terms achieved through legislation than through industry self-regulation or market evolution because courts have regarded legislation as the product of a democratic process and therefore prima facie in society's best interests. Schemes of uniform contracts, on the other hand, have to some courts and commentators looked like a property scheme imposed by private companies for their own interests instead of by the government for the interest of all. Because such sets of terms are dictated by one party rather than arrived at by negotiation between parties, they have been dubbed *contracts of adhesion*, or take-it-or-leave-it contracts. Courts in some circumstances have not considered them effective in creating contractual commitment on the part of the takers and have refused to enforce them.

There is some fuzziness about the definition of a contract of adhesion. Two basic characteristics often mentioned are that they are (1) standard forms that are perceived as (2) being imposed on people. It is clear, at least, that these contracts seem suspect on the issue of consent. When one set of terms becomes standard in an industry, so that the buyer cannot purchase a product without those terms, it is hard for many observers to consider that the buyer has chosen to be bound by those terms.

In reality, as many economic analysts have pointed out, the situation is more complicated. The terms themselves can be seen as a product the consumer is buying or part of the package the consumer is buying (product plus terms). If all buyers tend to choose these terms, then their ubiquity means nothing more than that they have won out in a free market. A number of suboptimal scenarios are possible, however, such as cartelization or an inefficient equilibrium in which lack of information on the part of consumers causes standardization on an inferior product. Deciding whether any given widespread standardized contract represents either lack of choice or market failure is not any easier than deciding whether any given piece of legislation is rent-seeking or in the public interest. In the face of this complexity, courts are likely to conclude that the more the terms seem onerous to the court, the less likely they are to be the result of buyer choice.

As mentioned earlier, I believe that the circumstances of electronic commerce may cause standard forms to emerge. For a large proportion of transactions, individual negotiation will not be cost-effective.[5] Another way to negotiate is to use a set of standard terms that have been tested and found workable. By *tested* I mean that some influential entity (whether private, public, or a mixture) in various high-profile jurisdictions has separated appropriate terms from those the entity deems unreasonable. Industry then learns to work with what is available and known to be enforceable, just as it learns to work with available technology. There is a feedback loop as more players become familiar with the terms (and therefore do not want to use different ones) and more courts or other entities validate them because they are prevalent.

The normal pressures of capitalism give industries a powerful incentive to make global electronic commerce work. Especially in the business-to-business (B2B) model, those who don't make it work will be dinosaurs. In other words, there is a strong incentive for industries desiring global commerce to coordinate among themselves, either explicitly or tacitly, to achieve standard sets of tested terms. It is orders of magnitude less expensive to do this in the online world, where everyone can see and download everyone else's

---

5. It is important to note, however, that individual negotiation is or soon will be potentially economically feasible in many consumer transactions where it has not been before. Web contracts could allow users to check a box and pay extra if they desired litigation rather than arbitration, litigation in their home state rather than in Los Angeles, and so on. In principle such customized contracts could be administered by specialized third parties, similar to precursors in the off-line world such as extended warranties on electronic equipment or automobiles. It remains to be seen whether there would be any market demand for such contractual customization. If customization did catch on, it might raise some policy problems of its own: firms might offer only the most minimal consumer protections in their basic contracts, and it might turn out that only wealthier and/or better-educated consumers would be willing or able to pay for better terms.

terms. The good ones will propagate quickly. At the same time, achieving coordination through governmental promulgation of standards is more difficult because the market is global. For these reasons, I believe firms probably have a better chance of coordinating to achieve standards than territorial sovereigns have of achieving legislative harmonization through diplomacy and trade wars. This means that difficult questions will arise regarding to what extent those sovereigns' rules of law can be contracted around; the answers will likely depend on whose law governs the decision. If the Disney contract imposing waiver of "all so-called moral rights" were brought before a court in France by a French citizen, the French court might find French rules about moral rights to be important enough not to enforce the terms in the contract that select the law of California and Los Angeles as the sole forum. A customary set of workable terms would have to avoid using terms like this, which would be repugnant in some important markets. I suspect that industry may well learn to do this.

As I mentioned earlier, another reason the world of on-line commerce may be organized largely by sets of standardized terms is that such terms will work better with machine-made contracts. B2B will remain a substantial proportion of electronic commerce, and it will make significant the use of machine-made contracts. If the use of machine-made contracts helps drive players to settle on sets of standard terms, then, because of the feedback effect mentioned above, there may well be an advantage to using the same terms for people-made contracts as well. The standard terms that machines can handle may become ubiquitous.

The traditional picture of contract makes many people feel that standard terms lack consent. If the world of on-line contract turns out to be more standardized—or more obviously standardized— than the world of off-line contract, the world of on-line contract will be troubling from the point of view that holds consent requisite for binding obligation to arise. We can expect commentators to point with alarm at "private" legislation through standardized contracts.

Excluded Terms

Public Policy Constraints on Contract

Developed legal systems do not enforce contracts that purport to relinquish basic human rights, such as one's freedom, one's right to bodily integrity, or one's right to vote. Beyond these basics, each legal system has a range of things that are off-limits to contract for public policy reasons, for example, contracts for sexual services or contracts waiving liability for one's own gross negligence.

Beyond the basics, there is no clear-cut best way to structure such public policy limitations on contract. They vary from place to place. We can assume that the kinds of terms that will look suspect to many judges are those that have people giving up important human rights or important legal rights. Human rights that might be held nonwaivable could include privacy (in Europe) or free speech (in the United States). Legal rights might include the right to seek redress of grievances (which would include the right to seek redress in a convenient forum).

Other kinds of terms may look suspect in their economic context. If a standard set of terms is widespread and/or promulgated by a dominant firm, it may be considered not to be a valid contract, as I mentioned above; but even where a standard set of terms is considered a valid contract, certain terms within it could still be invalidated because they are anticompetitive or conflict with other goals of the legal system.

Preemption

Related to the tough policy issue of what things are off-limits even if parties agree to them, there is, in the United States, a complex legal issue that goes by the name of *preemption*. The issue of preemption figures prominently in U.S. views about contracting around the provisions of other legal regimes, especially intellectual property.

Preemption, an artifact of federalism, refers to the trumping of state law by federal law. The supremacy clause of the U.S. Constitution provides that federal law is the supreme law of the land, anything in state law to the contrary notwithstanding. Under this doctrine, if federal law provides that the patent term is twenty years, California, for example, may not declare that in California it will be twenty-five. Although this hypothetical example is an easy case, there are large gray areas and many hard cases.

Preemption has proved particularly difficult in the field of intellectual property. The main intellectual property regimes in the United States are created by federal law, under the constitutional power granted to Congress to establish rights for authors and inventors (in the case of patent and copyright) and the power granted to Congress to regulate interstate commerce (in the case of trademark). Certain areas of state law (particularly trade secrets, right of publicity, misappropriation, and unfair competition) bump up against what is set forth in the federal regimes. The U.S. Supreme Court held that patent law precluded a cause of action under state misappropriation law for copying an unpatented item of manufacture. The court said (I'm paraphrasing), "It's patent or nothing; you can't get patentlike protection under state law where the federal law won't grant it to you."[6] A later Supreme Court, however, held that patent law did not preempt state trade secret law even for

6. *Sears, Roebuck & Co. v. Stiffel Co.*, 376 U.S. 225 (1964).

items that could have been patented but weren't.[7] The Supreme Court has also been somewhat permissive with respect to state supplementation of the federal copyright regime.[8] On the other hand, a state law that tried to curtail federal copyright would surely be struck down.

The U.S. courts' preemption decisions form a fuzzy picture at best. The rough pattern is that supplementation or enlargement of the scope of federal intellectual property rights will more often be allowed, whereas curtailing them will more often be disallowed. One main way of enlarging propertization is through contract: the parties agree to alter the background intellectual property scheme so that one party has more rights than the law would otherwise grant.[9] Will such contracts be enforceable—particularly if they are uniform and widespread?

Many of them will be enforceable, but perhaps not all. Of course, parties must be allowed to structure their deals in such a way as to alter their intellectual property rights, most of the time. But in the context of widespread standardized sets of terms, if all intellectual property rights are merely default rules, the structure of intellectual property rights will end up deviating greatly from what the lawmakers intended. The intellectual property structure, and the residual public domain, will instead be that which is promulgated by the contract drafters. Many observers consider that result problematic.

U.S. law, or at least its rhetoric, posits that intellectual property law is the result of a giant balancing analysis. In this balancing, rights are granted to creators solely to the extent necessary to

---

7. *Kewanee v. Bicron*, 416 U.S. 470 (1974).

8. *Goldstein v. California*, 412 U.S. 546 (1973).

9. Although the question arises under the doctrine of preemption in the United States, the same policy question (minus the federalism complications) is present everywhere. Are the provisions of the intellectual property scheme waivable at will? If so, what becomes of the intellectual property scheme and its policy basis?

achieve the correct incentive structure to draw forth the optimal amount of new information and invention. In fact, some analysts argue that it would be unconstitutional for Congress to create broader rights than necessary to achieve the optimal amount of innovation. In this balancing model, the purpose of the government's granting and maintaining intellectual property rights cannot come to fruition without a large store of information on which creators can freely draw to create new works (a public domain). In this model, therefore, problems are raised by state schemes that supplement the federal grants of intellectual property rights because these schemes distort the balance that Congress is supposed to have carefully created. They diminish the scope of the public domain that Congress is said to have intended. Schemes of contracts diminishing the scope of the public domain may count as such a state scheme because it is the state law of contract on which they rest.

ProCD v. Zeidenberg, discussed earlier in the context of contract formation, seemed to say that contracts will not count as a state scheme open to preemption. Judge Easterbrook reasoned that a contract is between two parties, so it can never be equivalent to a rule of intellectual property applicable to everyone. Thus the contract was not preempted. The logic of the reasoning seems to mean that no contract that altered any intellectual property rule would be preempted. (Arguably, Judge Easterbrook's opinion didn't quite go this far since he allowed that such contracts might be disallowed if they were clearly anticompetitive.)

Reasoning that contract law must be allowed to vary all intellectual property rules at all times, simply because contracts bind only two parties, is controversial. The idea is that the two parties consider themselves better off or they would not have entered into the contract. But to this we must add the implicit assumption that the rest of the world is not worse off. Some contracts in the digital networked environment fit this description. Many, however, do not. If a term increasing the property rights of a firm or industry is uniform and widespread, and especially if it stems from a dominant firm, it may entail significant negative externalities.

Jurisdiction and Choice of Law

If the fine print on a web site says that it is governed entirely by the law of California and that all legal action must take place in Los Angeles, is that a contract that the user is or should be bound to?

Consider first the legal situation in the absence of such a contract. It is hard to know where parties and transactions are "located" in the global networked environment, which means it is hard to know whose law applies and whose courts will take jurisdiction to enforce that law. Personal jurisdiction in states in the United States depends upon the reach of each state's "long-arm" statute, as that reach is limited by constitutional standards of due process and fair play. The test most often used is that the defendant must have minimum contacts with a state in order to be haled into court in that state. Does running a commercial web site that can be accessed by people in every state subject the site owner to being sued in every state? Under U.S. law, the answer is most likely yes for sites that are interactive with customers, especially if they ship goods to customers; at that point the site owner most likely will be held to have purposely availed itself of the law of the customer's state by transacting business "in" that state.

The situation is more complicated for multinational transactions, partly because each country's courts may think their own residents have a right to adjudication in their own courts and not those of some other country. The situation becomes even more complicated when the issue of choice of law is considered. Courts often use an interest analysis to decide choice of law questions (i.e., the law that will govern the transaction is that of the jurisdiction that has the most interest in having its law prevail). The question of choice of law is technically independent from the questions of jurisdiction, but in practice it is not completely separate. For example, if a court in France decides that California law governs a transaction, it may also decide that jurisdiction in California is proper rather than try to apply California law itself.

The traditional law on these matters, with its dependence on territorial sovereignty and complicated rules of comity and interest, is dysfunctional for global commerce. What is to be done? Can the situation be cured by contract? Can Disney really make California law govern any transaction involving its web site, and can it really restrict its venue to Los Angeles?

Choice of forum clauses and choice of law clauses may well work in many cases. They have often been found valid in negotiated contracts between commercial entities, in other words, in old-fashioned contracts that more or less fit the picture of a meeting of the minds between equals. To some courts, however, such clauses are problematic in "contracts" that consumers may not even know about. They may be less problematic in the United States than elsewhere, at least for forum selection, because the U.S. Supreme Court enforced a forum selection clause in a form ticket against a consumer, albeit one that was presumed to have had notice of the clause.[10] Nevertheless, if a consumer in France wanted to sue Dis-

---

10. *Carnival Cruise Lines, Inc. v. Shute*, 499 U.S. 585 (1991). In this case the plaintiffs, who resided in the state of Washington, bought tickets for a cruise. The tickets contained a form contract that included a clause limiting litigation to Florida. The contract was contained in fine print in an appendix, but the ticket said on its face, "Subject to Conditions of Contract on Last Pages Important! Please Read Contract—on Last Pages 1, 2, 3." The plaintiffs in their legal argument conceded that they had notice of the clause; instead, they contested reasonableness on the basis that the clause was not the product of negotiation between the parties. In upholding the validity of the clause, the court said:

> Including a reasonable forum clause in a form contract of this kind well may be permissible for several reasons: First, a cruise line has a special

ney and brought suit in a French court, it is certainly not clear that the French court would honor the "contract" and send its own aggrieved citizen to Los Angeles to be judged by California law.

Conclusion

In this chapter I have outlined five problems for contract in the networked digital environment. Progress is being made on the problem of authentication, but the other four problems remain difficult. The advent of the digital era has exacerbated the issues posed by contracts of adhesion and standardized forms. Courts have not arrived at a stable way of treating shrink-wrap licenses, and the proliferation of analogous purported contracts in e-commerce makes the issue more urgent. Machine-to-machine contracts and viral contracts present new legal problems. What will courts do when confronted by parties asking not to be bound by deals made by their computers or by clauses passed on to them through a chain of distribution?

---

interest in limiting the fora in which it potentially could be subject to suit. Because a cruise ship typically carries passengers from many locales, it is not unlikely that a mishap on a cruise could subject the cruise line to litigation in several different fora. . . . Additionally, a clause establishing ex ante the forum for dispute resolution has the salutary effect of dispelling any confusion about where suits arising from the contract must be brought and defended, sparing litigants the time and expense of pretrial motions to determine the correct forum and conserving judicial resources that otherwise would be devoted to deciding those motions.

Finally, it stands to reason that passengers who purchase tickets containing a forum clause like that at issue in this case benefit in the form of reduced fares reflecting the savings that the cruise line enjoys by limiting the fora in which it may be sued. (593–94)

Forum selection clauses will still be subject to judicial scrutiny for fundamental fairness and can still be set aside on a showing of genuine inconvenience to the plaintiff. Also, of course, this case refers to a dispute between two U.S. parties and does not shed much light on how a dispute between a U.S. party and a non-U.S. party would be viewed.

If commerce is to be global, we will need more certainty about which terms in contracts are enforceable, and perhaps we will need largely uniform sets of terms whose enforceability in ordinary circumstances has been determined. To achieve that level of certainty of enforceability, the background rules of contract will also need to be more uniform than they are now. It remains uncertain how that level of uniformity will be achieved globally.

Significant obstacles now stand in the way of achieving what is needed in the way of legal infrastructure to enable global e-commerce. To move beyond the present crisis for contract, business and political leaders will have to overcome these obstacles. In my opinion, the obstacles are not primarily technical or economic; they are primarily ideological. They are primarily in our heads.

One obstacle is the perceived problematic nature of standardized contracts and the widespread assumption that mere standardization signifies oppression. Each case of standardization has to be investigated in its economic circumstances in order to understand whether it is efficiency-enhancing or not. At least economically speaking, standardization that emerges from the market or from industry coordination is not different from standardization that emerges from legislation. Without more understanding of the circumstances that give rise to any particular instance of standardization, there should not be a presumption in favor of legislated standardization and against market-emergent standardization. Questions to ask include, prominently, whether a dominant firm or a cartel is able to forclose choices that consumers would otherwise wish to make.

On the other hand, it will not be satisfactory to stop here and say that the legal system should have no standardized system for evaluating instances of standardization. For the same reason that some degree of technical standardization is necessary in order for commerce to function, some degree of legal standardization is also needed, which includes a standardized way of evaluating instances of standardization. Finding such a system for evaluating standardized contrcts is an important task we now face. It will be important to begin this task without the assumptions underlying the traditional distinction between legislative standards and market-emergent standards.

Another obstacle is the liberal ideological complex of values involving the traditional ideal of contractual consent and the commitment—at least in the United States—to "private ordering" over "regulation." In modern commerce, even before the digital era, the traditional ideal of consent—the meeting of the minds between two autonomous humans—has become more and more attentuated. Transactions have come to be governed by terms that parties cannot read or do not care to read, perhaps because their time would not be efficiently spent reading them; contractual terms have come to be considered, at least by economists, as part of the product, a package deal, rather than something separate. The choice to buy the product blends into the "choice" to "accept" the terms that come with it. The attentuation of consent in on-line contracts is thus not a radical shift but rather further evolution along these lines.

That being so, how can we hang on to the liberal value of autonomous consent as we move into the era of digital commerce? If the only choice is whether or not to buy the product-plus-terms, we can focus our attention on preservation of individual autonomy at that point. One way to do this, of course, is to make sure that the marketplace offers a full array of competing products-plus-terms. But to some extent this goal of diversity is in conflict with the efficiencies of standardization. Also, depending on the economic circumstances, preservation of market diversity may require aggressive antitrust enforcement or other types of state implementation of competition policy. Electronic self-enforcement systems—digital rights management mechnisms—will be suspect from the point of view of competition policy if they lock up information under onerous terms and the information is not available elsewhere under other terms.

This market solution implies as a background condition the requirement that products-plus-terms can be fully disclosed to buyers, so that buyers will know what they are choosing when they choose whether or not to buy. Yet this is the implication that modern commerce cannot, or at least cannot often, fulfill. Even if sellers do not lie about the underlying product or the terms, it is not efficient or even possible for buyers to take the time to understand all this information. Thus, policymakers end up having to make decisions about what information it is important to draw buyers' attention to in order to preserve their autonomy. As these decisions are make, policymakers will be drawing up the parameters of the infrastructure of contract. Policymakers must face questions like these: Do we believe that buyers must be made fully aware when redress of grievances is limited to a specific venue or limited to a short time period? Do we believe that buyers must be made fully aware of their potential liability if they warrant intellectual property rights in posted messages? And so on.

In the off-line world many products are not left to the free market for various reasons, even with full disclosure. Airline safety is an example; we don't leave it up to consumers to purchase the amount of airline safety they want. One way to explain imposition of regulatory safety standards is the fact that no one expects consumers to understand and evaluate the various risks to their safety engendered by various maintenance practices, cargo practices, security practices, and so on, even if somehow they could all be fully disclosed, coupled with the magnitude of the loss if the risk is wrongly evaluated. There may be similar need for regulatory structure in the on-line world. These are the kinds of questions policymakers will need to consider: Can we expect consumers to weigh the efficacy of the practices of a certificate authority? Can we expect consumers to understand and evaluate properly the risks of allowing their personal data to be aggregated by commercial enterprises?

To be able to consider these questions properly, we cannot start with a distaste for anything called *regulation*. We must remember that the borderline between "private ordering" and "regulation" has always been in the eye of the beholder. It shifts depending on whether the observer believes that a particular government activity fosters an orderly functioning market, for example, by correcting market failure, or detracts from it, for example, by implementing a rent-seeking scheme. Regulation is needed to make private ordering work, such as when we promulgate rules policing transactions for fraud and coercion and when we promulgate rules for adequate disclosure of certain kinds of terms. As we work on the legal infrastructure needed to make the potential of global e-commerce a reality, it would be well not to be derailed by ideological labels.

Appendix:
Symposium Participants

Alan Austin   *Managing Partner, Wilson, Sonsini, Goodrich & Rosati*

George Bell   *Chief Executive Officer, Excite@Home*

Joseph Costello   *Chairman and Managing Director, Think 3*

Mary J. Cronin   *Professor of Management, Boston College*

William H. Davidow   *General Partner, Mohr, Davidow Ventures*

Susan J. Duggan   *Chief Executive Officer, Silicon Valley World Internet Center*

Charles Geschke   *President and Chairman, Adobe Systems*

Andrew S. Grove   *Chairman of the Board, Intel Corporation*

Bill Harris   *President and CEO, Intuit*

Nicholas Imparato   *Symposium Chair, Research Fellow, Hoover Institution*

Daniel Leemon *Executive Vice President and Chief Strategy Officer, Charles Schwab Corporation*

Charles E. McLure Jr. *Senior Fellow, Hoover Institution*

Pete Montgomery *Policy Analyst, Hoover Institution*

David Pottruck *President and Co-CEO, Charles Schwab Corporation*

Margaret Jane Radin *William Benjamin Scott and Luna M. Scott Professor of Law, Stanford University*

Pamela Samuelson *Professor, School of Information Management and Systems, University of California, Berkeley*

Gideon Sasson *President, Electronic Brokerage, Charles Schwab Corporation*

Charles Schwab *Chairman and Co-CEO, Charles Schwab Corporation*

Solveig Singleton *Director of Information Studies, Cato Institute*

Abraham D. Sofaer *George P. Shultz Senior Fellow in Foreign Policy and National Security, Hoover Institution; Professor (by courtesy), Stanford University Law School*

Ronald S. Weiner *Chief Executive Officer, PetNet*

Pete Wilson *Distinguished Visiting Fellow, Hoover Institution; Former Governor, State of California*

Jerry Yang *Cofounder and Chief Yahoo, Yahoo! Inc.*

Index

Abacus Direct, 8
advertising; personalization of messages in, 8
Advisory Commission on Electronic Commerce (ACEC): members of, 75; moratorium and, 105; no tax experts in, 75; proposal for reform for state sales and use tax by, 89, 91; radical simplification of sales and use tax discusses, 76; status quo and, 75
"Appeal for Fair and Equal Taxation of Electronic Commerce," 54–55, 108–113; de minimis rules for, 107; e-commerce not different from other businesses and, 106; origin-based tax not for, 107; remote sales/destination tax for, 106–107; simplification and unification with, 107
authentication: certificate authorities for, 120; digital signature as means of, 119; electronic, 119; European Union (EU) and, 119; fraud and, 119; progress on, 145; public key cryptography for, 119; signed, written form necessary for, 119

BBB*Online,* 36
behavior, on-line: hostage to technology, data, and, 9; individual's unawareness of recording of, 7–9, 39–44
Brandeis, Louis D., 3–4

cable: consumer protection in, 5; Internet privacy *vs.* privacy on, 27
Cable Communications Policy Act of 1984, 5
Carnival Cruise Lines, Inc. Shute, 144–45 note
catalog sales: checks *vs.* credit card for, 68
commerce: four way division of, 81 *figure*

Commission of the European Communities, 88
company(s): *See also* self-regulation; e-commerce; cooperative efforts with, 48, 137; customer trust of, 3, 15, 43; damage of reputation of, 46; develop of new structure in contracts of e-commerce, 118; economic self-interest for, 46; global, 137, 146; industry review boards for, 46–47; lack of voluntary compliance of self-regulation by, 33; large, 25; middle-size, 26, 45; multinational, 84–85; privacy and, 25; privacy seal programs for, 35–37; responsibility of, 44–45; small, 25–26, 45; solving issues through expertise of, 25
consumer information: average user shares great amount of, 38; banks, credit card companies and mail houses affect on, 6; citizen review of, 5; data collection of, 4, 9, 47; destruction of unnecessary, 5; difficulty for opt-out choices in, 41–42; disclosure with, 3, 16; education campaign and, 39, 42; exchange services/compensation for, 12, 23, 44–45; explosion in, 4–5, 6; intrusion from, 4–5, 9; as personal property, 12; positive motivation for, 37; profiling of, 15; revenue and, 27; tracking of, 39–44
consumer protection: *See also* European Directive on; Data Protection; regulations; self-regulation; access for, 29, 30–31, 32; business benefits from, 45; data collection blocking options for, 43; enforcement for, 29, 31–32; false sense of security with, 26; laws for, 5–6, 11; NetCoalition for, 47; notice and choice in, 28, 30, 32, 37–38, 41; Online Privacy Alliance (OPA) value for, 32, 34